Yeshua in Context

The Life and Times of Yeshua the Messiah

Derek Leman

Published by:
Mount Olive Press
Post Office Box 659
Stone Mountain, GA 30086
mountolivepress.com

ISBN 978-0-9747814-4-0
First printing 2010.
Library of Congress Control Number: 2010909973
This book is printed on archival quality paper.

TABLE OF CONTENTS

1   The Real Yeshua 1
Mark 1:1-20

2   The Unexpected Yeshua 9
Luke 4:14-30

3   The Heralding Yeshua 17
Mark 1:16-45

4   Yeshua as Exorcist 25
Mark 1:23-28; Luke 11:19-20; 13:32

5   Yeshua as Healer 33
Mark 5:21-43; Luke 7:22; 10:18

6   The Messianic Secret 39
Mark 8:22-35

7   The Temple Cleansing 47
John 2:13-22

8   The Handwashing Dispute 55
Mark 7:1-23

9   The Prodigal Story 63
     Luke 15:11-32

10   Beatitudes of Hope 71
     Matthew 5:1-12

11   Seeds and Fruit 81
     Mark 4:1-20

12   The Wicked Tenants. 89
     Mark 12:1-12

13   Born from Above. 99
     John 3:1-21

14   Messiah's Trial 113
     Mark 14:53-65

15   Crucifixion Irony. 123
     Mark 15:16-39

16   The Living and Present Lord. 133
     Luke 24:36-53

17   The True Vine. 143
     John 15:1-17

BIBLIOGRAPHY

MAIN COMMENTARIES CITED

Brown, Raymond E. *The Gospel According to John I-XII.* 1966. Reprint, New Haven: Yale University Press, 2006.

-----. *The Gospel According to John XIII-XXI.* 1970. Reprint, New Haven: Yale University Press, 2008.

-----. *The Death of the Messiah: From Gethsemane to the Grave: A Commentary on the Passion Narratives in the Four Gospels, Vol. 1.* New York: Doubleday, 1994.

Collins, Adela Yarbro. Attridge, Harold W., ed. *Mark.* Minneapolis: Fortress Press, 2007.

Davies, W.D. and Allison, Dale C. *Matthew: A Shorter Commentary.* New York: T&T Clark International, 2004.

Johnson, Luke Timothy. *The Gospel of Luke.* Collegeville: The Liturgical Press, 1991.

Levertoff, Paul Philip. *Love in the Messianic Age.* Marshfield: Vine of David, 2009 (original edition: London: Episcopal Hebrew Christian Church Publications, 1923).

MAIN HISTORICAL BOOKS CITED

Evans, Craig A. and Wright, N.T. *Jesus, The Final Days: What Really Happened.* Louisville: Westminster John Knox Press, 2009.

Elliott, Mark Adam. *The Survivors of Israel.* Grand Rapids: Eerdmans, 2000.

McKnight, Scot. *Jesus and His Death: Historiography, the Historical Jesus, and Atonement Theory.* Waco: Baylor University Press, 2005.

Sanders, E.P. *The Historical Figure of Jesus.* London: Penguin, 1993 (1995 Penguin Books edition).

-----. *Judaism, Practice and Belief: 63 BCE - 66 CE.* Philadelphia: Trinity Press International, 1992.

Vermes, Geza. *Jesus the Jew.* Philadelphia: Fortress Press, 1981.

Wright, N.T. *The New Testament and the People of God.* Minneapolis: Fortress Press, 1992.

-----. *Jesus and the Victory of God.* Minneapolis: Fortress Press, 1996.

OTHER WORKS CITED

Betz, Hans Dieter. *Essays on the Sermon on the Mount.* Minneapolis: Fortress, 2009.

Bock, Darrell. *Luke, Volume 1.* Grand Rapids: Baker, 1994.

Charlesworth, James. *The Old Testament Pseudepigrapha, Vol. 1.* New York: Doubleday, 1983.

Ehrman, Bart. *Jesus, Interrupted: Revealing the Hidden Contradictions in the Bible (And Why We Don't Know About Them).* New York: HarperOne, 2010.

Ehrman, Bart. *God's Problem: How the Bible Fails to Answer Our Most Important Question—Why We Suffer.* New York: HarperOne, 2008.

Gaventa, Beverly Roberts and Hays, Richard B., eds. *Seeking the Identity of Jesus: A Pilgrimage.* Grand Rapids: Eerdmans, 2008.

Motyer, J.A. *The Prophecy of Isaiah: An Introduction & Commentary.* Downer's Grove: IVP Academic, 1993.

Chapter 1

The Real Yeshua
Mark 1:2-20

Who is the real Yeshua? There have been different ways to pursue this question and different motives for doing it. Some have been on a quest for the "historical Jesus." Others have tried to delve the depths of the "Christ of faith." What does "real" mean, why do we want to find the real Yeshua, and what would the search look like?

Knowing the limitless differences in people—varied paths in life, divergent influences—no quest book or historical investigation or thoughtful sermon will universally satisfy. Yet if there is one universal in the quest for knowing Yeshua, it is something universal to all areas of human study. I am talking about the idea of story. The real Yeshua exists in stories, just like every person we know in person, through conversation, or through reading.

Ask yourself about your closest friend, your spouse, your child. You know them also through stories and some of the stories include you within them while others are independent of you. Some of the stories you know and some you only wonder about. How did this person I love become who they are now? How do they see themselves? How do others see them?

We know Yeshua in stories. Some are the stories we read in the Bible. Countless other stories overlap and intersect—stories from Josephus the historian or Philo the Jewish philosopher or numerous other ancient writers. Some of the stories are not told in words, but in stones and artifacts, remains of the past.

We can ask who the real Yeshua is by considering stories. Perhaps the more we know, the clearer our picture might be. We have so many

1

questions: did the real Yeshua exist, work miracles, emerge alive from the tomb and so on. We hear stories told by modern interpreters and wonder if they are real: Jesus was a political revolutionary, a cynic sage, a Galilean healer, a Pharisee, a prophet-Messiah and so on.

We have our own stories, our own encounters with the story of Jesus. Some are positive and some negative, some we believe and some we don't, some we consider reliable and others unreliable. Jesus may have been presented to us in childhood in inspiring or frightening ways. We may have experienced different facets of the story of Jesus, the story told in stained glass windows inspiring awe and faith on the one hand and the story told in "scientific-historical" terms on the other.

It is likely of consequence to us how we regard the many stories of Jesus and how we navigate through them to form an idea of the real Yeshua. We know that our choice about what stories to believe could amount to life and death for us, especially in those moments when we take life and death seriously. They could mean the satisfaction of intellectual curiosity or a sense of genuine experience or a decision about a path in life. We may think of ourselves as followers of Yeshua, seekers of the truth about Yeshua, skeptics, cynics, or downright disbelievers. In one way or another the story matters deeply to us.

Ancient Stories

While not dismissing the importance of personal stories or contemporary stories, most of us would agree that the real Yeshua is best sought through ancient stories. Whoever the real Yeshua is, and however closely we may or may not be able to discover him, we can guess that less genuine depictions have grown over time. Foreign influences on our image of a Jewish man from the first century have crept in. While we may believe that some aspects of Yeshua are timeless, others are time-bound.

We should be rightly suspicious of any teller of these stories, even if they are ancient. Every telling of a story is influenced by the one telling it. I do not pretend that my selection of stories to tell is neutral or objective. I am a rabbi in Messianic Judaism, a Judaism that believes in and follows Yeshua. I bring to the investigation a definite bias toward a view of Yeshua as the one sent by the Father and also a bias toward Yeshua as an Israelite (as opposed to the European-looking Jesus). So the stories as I will tell them are going to point in these general directions.

In a way, my biases are similar to those in the gospels (Matthew, Mark, Luke, and John). Their stories about Yeshua are told with the end of the story in mind. The Yeshua of the gospels is understood even from birth as the Yeshua who will die and rise again, earthly and heavenly, human and divine. Every instance they record has overtones of the larger story.

It's a bit like the way we write about heroes. The incidents surrounding their birth and upbringing take on a new meaning because of something heroic we know about them. The later story goes back to the earlier ones and adds depth that was unseen before the heroic deeds or profound discoveries that made them heroes.

Not all of the storytellers of the life and times of Yeshua the Messiah are followers and admirers. There are other ancient storytellers who illuminate the life of Yeshua for other reasons. Josephus tells stories about Israel and Rome, stories about Israel for the benefit of Romans who want to understand the Jewish psyche, and stories about the war between Rome and the Israelites. In the process we learn a lot about Yeshua's world, about Herod, the Roman governors and emperors, Pharisees, Sadducees, Essenes, and more. Unknown apocalyptic writers tell us about the hopes and expectations of groups of the faithful and even the mystical. Dead Sea scrolls written by Essene sectarians tell us of other Jewish ideas and open a new window on the world of Yeshua's time.

The advantage of turning to ancient storytellers is that they precede various events which may have twisted our image of Yeshua. They wrote before the sad history of Christian anti-Semitism. They wrote before the many Judaisms of Yeshua's time were forgotten. While their worldviews cannot be said to match the worldview of Yeshua, they had more in common with him than we do.

Our story and the ancient stories—they intersect in complex and innumerable ways. Listening to them affects us. Some of them we believe outright. Some we believe in part, while others we doubt. All of them offer us a window into meaning, piercing the mystery and the veil. It's our deepest desire, to know what is beyond.

A Foundational Yeshua Story

Some stories about Yeshua promise to give us the bigger picture more than others do. It is with these kind of stories that I will begin. In every chapter I will tell a story and examine some background from the sources we have about Yeshua's life and times, his deeds and sayings. My goal is to explore the larger issues of his aims, his character, his ideas.

The story approach is frustrating for some. Our times condition us to look for summaries and bottom lines, bullet points and timeless truths. Just give us the skinny. In our inundation of information, we rarely take time to smell the air, taste the savor, feel the movement, hear the wind, and see the mystery.

There are truths and there are experiences. The best truths are experienced. The storied approach is about experience as well as learning. Learning through experience lasts while briskly skimmed factoids dissolve.

Truth is multi-faceted, an array of ideas almost contradictory at times. No person is defined by a handful of characteristics. Facets overlap and compete. Yeshua is far from the simplest character you will meet. The large-picture stories are a beginning.

Near the beginning of Mark, we encounter one of these core stories about Yeshua. Historically it has gotten less attention than it should. The Yeshua in this story seems a lot like John the Baptist or Elijah and a lot less like the Christ of many works of art decorating the walls of churches. Few people associate Yeshua with the image of a Jewish prophet in the desert, but that is how his work began.

The players are the disciples of John the Baptist as well as the crowds who have come from the cities to the Jordan River in the

Judean desert. A whole movement has been going on for some time out here. This movement has been about the return of prophecy to Israel after a very long silence. The people of Judea and Galilee are persuaded that they live in momentous times. The prophet John has been immensely popular.

The hills of the Judean desert are hard-baked, like John, and the sun scorches in the daytime. But by the river there is life, a long oasis snaking through the hardened wilderness. Likewise, in this hardened prophet, with his camel hair garment, there is a message of hope and life. Yet at the height of his popularity, John runs afoul of the Herodian family and is arrested. The disciples and crowds waiting for God's next move wonder how the movement will continue with John in prison.

Yeshua brings the movement of John to a new place. Geographically, he brings it to Galilee in the north. Spiritually, he brings it to deeper realizations than John's simple message ever could. Many of John's disciples are from Galilee, including a group of fishermen from the great lake in Galilee. Some of the disciples of John already know Yeshua as the one John spoke about. John said Yeshua would be mightier. Surprisingly, perhaps, Yeshua begins with a message the same as John's, "The time is fulfilled and the kingdom of God is near. Repent and believe the gospel" (Mark 1:15). How will Yeshua bring this eager movement further along? What will he do with all these disciples?

The story of John and Yeshua should bring to mind an older story, from the Hebrew scriptures. Israel had already experienced a prophet like John about 850 years earlier, the prophet Elijah. And a greater one came after him, one who raised more disciples and worked more miracles, the prophet Elisha. Elijah and Elisha had built a movement of disciples, the sons of the prophets, who were eager to see renewal in Israel.

Just like the older story, Yeshua gathers disciples right after he starts declaring the coming kingdom. Mark's telling of the story gives no hint that these disciples already knew Yeshua from the Judean desert and the movement associated with John. The powerful calling of disciples by Yeshua is so sudden and drastic, it is as if men were willing to suddenly drop everything and follow this Elisha, this prophet-successor.

Prophet and Disciples

What is Yeshua planning to do with the band of disciples he is gathering? He talks about catching people, apparently winning their hearts for something. Based on the summary of Yeshua's message, that it is about the soon-coming kingdom, it seems Yeshua is building a renewal movement.

The work Yeshua is doing is clearly dangerous. After all, John is in prison, held by powers with the ability to harm prophets. Talk of a kingdom immediately brings danger from those who already regard themselves as the holders of kingdom authority in Judea, Samaria, and Galilee.

The tetrarch of Galilee is Herod Antipas, son of Herod the Great. His power is nearly absolute. The Herodian administration in Galilee will not be happy to hear about kingdoms and renewal movements.

The power behind Antipas is Rome and in Judea the kingdom is administered by Pilate, the Prefect or Governor. Rome typically rounds up revolutionaries. If these revolutionaries have been violent, the leaders and their followers are all executed. If they have not been violent, just the leaders are arrested and killed. Rome will hear nothing of coming kingdoms.

Just like Elijah and Elisha in ancient days, Yeshua is doing something that threatens the current power structures. The whole country has been boiling toward revolution and war anyway. And now Yeshua is speaking of a change in the kingdom and is drawing disciples to himself. Who is this prophet? What will his renewal be about?

Connecting to Our Story

Many believe the stories of Yeshua connect to our own story. He is not merely a historical figure who was doing something back then but whose activity is a thing of the past.

What is this kingdom which Yeshua said was near? There are indications from later stories about Yeshua that the calling of disciples was not just for his own time. The disciples were to pass down the call to others and pass it on from generation to generation.

Considering this possible connection, we wonder what it might mean for us in our time. Antipas and Rome are long gone. Yet have the ideas of God's kingdom passed away also?

This early in our look at Yeshua stories, we can only wonder. Has the kingdom which Yeshua said was near actually appeared? If so, why doesn't the world look like God's kingdom? Is discipleship under Yeshua today like discipleship then?

What is Yeshua's renewal movement about? Is the kingdom good news still? We find at the beginning that Yeshua was a prophet, a proclaimer of a change in power, of a turning of the ages. And this program of Yeshua is not passive, it is more than just waiting for God. But what shape would the activity of Yeshua's disciples take? And what would it look like for us to follow the movement as well?

It may take many stories to begin filling in answers to these questions. But already we know one thing Yeshua believed about preparing for the kingdom. He believed that repentance was the prerequisite.

Repentance is a well-known Jewish idea. It comes with a whole worldview behind it. Repentance assumes that there is a king and the king has subjects. The subjects of the king are responsible to know and obey the king's wishes. Yet the assumption of the Jewish worldview is that the subjects often fail the king, corporately and individually. Repentance is a subject much discussed in the prophets.

"Rend your hearts and not your garments," said Joel (2:13, RSV). "Seek good and not evil so you can live," said Amos (5:14). "O man, what is good, and what the Lord really wants from you: He wants you to promote justice, to be faithful and to live obediently before your God" said Micah (6:8).

Yeshua, the Israelite prophet, surely had something like this in mind. And so, right at the beginning, we see that Yeshua's movement is revolutionary, but not about war. We see it is about God, but God's people are expected to do something and not just wait. The more stories we will hear, the more it will become plain to us that Yeshua's revolution has a different code of ethics, an unexpected set of criteria. The difference between revolution and renewal is subtle and this may explain a lot of Yeshua's words and deeds. No wonder he said at his trial, "My kingship is not from the world" (John 18:36, RSV).

Chapter 2

The Unexpected Yeshua
Luke 4:14-30

What do we need to better understand the real Yeshua? We have to, whenever possible, cross the gap between now and then, between our time and his. Sometimes when we read a story about Yeshua sitting in our drywalled rooms at our wood and metal desks holding paper books in our plastic chairs, we feel the distance between then and now. What are we missing?

We are missing some stories, stories that Yeshua's hearers would have shared and understood. We need to know how the stories overlap, how they are connected. We need to understand the characters, the motives, the setting, and the expectations.

Yet we are not alone in our trouble grasping Yeshua. His own hearers had trouble grasping him as well. He represented the unexpected, the subversive. His own hearers were often unenthusiastic about following him, or even hostile. Often, from our comfortable chairs we have trouble understanding what moved Yeshua's critics so. Why were they so offended by him? What are we missing?

In Luke 4 we find another one of those core stories about Yeshua, much like the story we just considered from Mark 1. This is a story that gets at the essence of Yeshua, what his aims were, and how his audience reacted to him. It is the story of Yeshua coming to his hometown and speaking good news from Isaiah and then saying it all points to himself and what he is doing. It is a story of a bold claim, an unexpected idea of messianic mission, and a hometown crowd not happy with what they hear.

The Story as Foreshadowing

Luke places the story of Yeshua coming to his hometown out of order. He carefully notes that the story is being told out of order. What makes a writer put a story at the beginning of a narrative when it clearly comes later? The answer, quite simply, is that some stories are defining and belong near the beginning. They help interpret what comes later.

So, in Luke 4:14-15, we read of various adventures Yeshua had in Galilee. Many see and hear him. Many are amazed. A lot of excitement is building about this Yeshua. He works many wondrous deeds. But Luke doesn't tell us about them yet. He puts a later story first. It is his choice as a storyteller and just as we pay close attention to flashbacks and foreshadowings in movies, we should pay attention here.

This core story is found in Luke 4:16-30. It is Yeshua returning to his hometown. The story is told with gaps, it raises questions, it takes some preparation to understand.

Background: Isaiah's Anointed Conqueror

It helps before reading the story to know a bit about the texts Yeshua is going to read from the prophet Isaiah. Yeshua's hearers had an advantage. They were in synagogue. They heard Yeshua read from the scroll. When he claimed that they were looking at the fulfillment of Isaiah's words, they had some idea what Yeshua was talking about.

But what about the audience in Luke's time, the people he expected to read his gospel? They weren't at the Nazareth synagogue that day, just as we weren't. Luke, like the other gospel writers, expects his audience to be regularly immersed in the Torah and prophets. Luke expects his audience to be familiar. Many moderns are weak on their understanding of books like Isaiah. We are too often not the ideal readers Luke had in mind.

Yeshua is going to read from the last section of Isaiah, chapters 56-66, a section which has its own characteristics compared to the earlier two (chs. 1-39 and 40-55). In this last section, the prophet speaks again and again about an anointed conqueror, the Messiah come to heal the world at last (see *The Prophecy of Isaiah* by J.A. Motyer). It's not that talk of Messiah is new to this section, but that the focus is almost exclusively on the victory of Messiah and the completed work of healing and renewing.

We can get some clues from the Luke version of the story about what parts Yeshua read. Luke shortens the reading into its essence and leaves it to the reader to guess from where Yeshua read:

> The Spirit of the Lord is upon me,
>> because he has anointed me to proclaim good news to the poor.
>
> He has sent me to proclaim release to the captives
>> and the regaining of sight to the blind,
>
> to set free those who are oppressed,
>> to proclaim the year of the Lord's favor. (Luke 4:18-19).

We can tell from Luke's summary that Yeshua read either a selection of verses from Isaiah 58 and 61 or a longer reading that included these chapters. The summary in Luke contains a phrase from Isaiah 58:6 and several phrases from Isaiah 61:1-2.

Isaiah 58 is a sharp criticism of religious people who are completely missing God. It is about people who pray and keep some of God's commands while missing the greater will of God completely. They ask God, "Why have we fasted and you have not seen?" They believe their actions have earned them blessing, but they are missing the blessing.

God says, in essence, you worship me but you don't do what I want. You ignore injustice and suffering. You turn a cold eye to hunger and pain. In 58:6, he uses the line which Luke includes in his summary of Yeshua's reading, "to set at liberty the oppressed." God says if people were really following him, that's the kind of result that would be seen in Israel.

Isaiah 61 begins with a first person saying by the Anointed One, the conquering Messiah of Israel. He speaks of liberating, bringing good news, declaring a year of God's favor, and a day of vengeance. Yeshua, according to Luke's summary, did not focus on the year of God's vengeance. He focused on the year of God's favor, the liberation, the good news.

A Critique of His Generation

In other words, to a synagogue crowd in Israel, Yeshua read from Isaiah about misguided religion and the liberating Messiah who comes for the oppressed and the needy. He then said, "Today this scripture has been fulfilled even as you heard it being read" (vs. 21).

What did Yeshua mean? What might his audience have thought he meant? They had heard of his miracles in other parts of Galilee, but he had done none of them in Nazareth.

Here is where the story becomes revealing and also where the gaps raise questions for us as we read it. The first reaction of the audience seems positive, "all were speaking well of him." The second reaction is ambiguous, "Isn't this Joseph's son [who grew up right here]?" Do they mean this positively, proud of their local son who may be the Messiah? Or do they mean this negatively, scorning the idea that this kid they knew is now some great king coming to rescue Israel.

Matthew and Mark's versions focus on the negative reaction of the crowd. Luke seems to accentuate the initial positive reaction.

Yet, Yeshua, it would appear, has not come to be congratulated. His next words are combative, condemning. He says he expects his audience to quote a popular proverb, one found in a number of Greek and Roman writings from the time, perhaps well known in Israel as well (Bock 416, note 38). The idea behind the saying, "Doctor, heal yourself," is something like, "you make claims, now show us" or "first heal yourself and then we'll believe you can heal us."

Yeshua continues, denouncing his audience, and knows they are wondering, "If you are the liberator we are waiting for, why haven't you show us signs and miracles like we've seen elsewhere?" Yeshua assumes that his audience will not welcome him. No prophet is welcome in his hometown, he says.

He then goes on to some unusual examples from the shared stories of Israel. He speaks about days of great trouble in Israel when the prophet Elijah helped a widow in Sidon, a Gentile, and did not help the many widows in Israel. In another story, a leper from Syria came and got help from the prophet Elisha, while the many lepers in Israel did not get help.

The people become enraged. They try to throw him off a cliff. But God protects Yeshua. A sharp reader will note that Satan had earlier tempted him to throw himself off the Temple and let God rescue him. Yeshua refused then. But now, in what must be a miracle, Yeshua just walks through the crowd unharmed.

Yeshua's Message in Detail

The story leaves us with questions. What is the point of talking about prophets helping Gentiles while Israelites went without help? What so enraged his hometown audience?

The two clues to consider are: (1) the reading from Isaiah and (2) the stories of Elijah and Elisha as a critique of Yeshua's own generation.

The reading from Isaiah tell us two things. First, many people call on God for help but do not see what it is that God wants from them. Second, the messianic mission Yeshua is undertaking is not the one expected by his audience.

The Luke 4 story is about Yeshua's unexpected mission, the way he subverts the normal expectations of his generation. It is a story intended to help us see why Yeshua was rejected by his own closest people and accepted by others, those least expected. The Luke 4 story is about a Yeshua ironically rejected and yet ironically accepted at the same time. He is the hometown prophet rejected by his hometown. He is the king, rejected by the powerful, but embraced by the marginal. It is not only the leaders of Israel, so often criticized in the gospels and other Jewish writings of the time, but also many of the common people who reject Yeshua's teaching and purpose.

There are many passages about Messiah in Isaiah and the prophets. Many are about a king who conquers enemies of Israel and makes a Golden Age for his country. Yeshua's audience preferred that one particular narrative about Messiah, the one in which he brings the day of God's vengeance on Israel's enemies. That is the Yeshua his hometown crowd would have liked to see. When the first Jewish revolt started, less than forty years after Yeshua's time, the people of Galilee were among the rebels seeking to throw off Roman power. The beginnings of war, of the hoped for day of vengeance, were in the air even at the time Yeshua read the scroll in his hometown.

Yet, Yeshua did not focus on the day of vengeance, but the day of God's favor, the liberation of those trapped and the healing of those hurting. That too is a messianic task. It is just not the one people wanted most to see.

So, Yeshua spoke of unexpected people finding help and healing. This is not, as some have imagined, Luke denouncing Judaism in favor of the Christianity of his time (Luke's time is the generation after Yeshua). It is, rather, Luke explaining why the Yeshua movement of his time is missing some of those most expected to follow Messiah and why it includes some of those least expected to follow Messiah.

Luke didn't have to invent a story to make his point. He found it already in something Yeshua had done and said. Luke simply shaped his story in a way to make the point clear. People closest to Yeshua, his fellow Nazarenes, did not seek him out, just as many widows and lepers in Israel never sought out Elijah or Elisha. Gentiles from outside the land received help and healing from the great prophets while Israelites missed the blessing.

And people who sincerely call on God and pray to him can miss the point. Yes, even good Jews can fail to understand Messiah when he appears. He is the Messiah of the unexpected. He has more than one mission.

The Unexpected Context

Yeshua in his own context was a mismatch. At least that's how many people regarded him. Thousands came to see the wonder-worker doing miracles on Galilean hillsides, but after the cross and resurrection, there were only a little over a hundred following him.

Comparing the context of Yeshua to society then and now reveals a similar mismatch. People are still looking for self-centered deliverance. Yeshua offers healing to the world, the whole conglomeration of smelly, unpretty people most would rather ignore.

Yeshua as the ticket to a heavenly afterlife is all the Yeshua some people will consider. They are like the crowd seeking a warrior messiah, the bringer of a golden age. Others think Yeshua's whole story is fanciful. Miracles, it seems to them, are impossible. They are like the Nazareth crowd, among which Mark tells us Yeshua could not work miracles because of their unbelief (Mark 6:5).

But the liberation Yeshua says he offers is many things, all-encompassing, world-changing. The correct response, according to Yeshua, is the one found amongst the Gentiles in the Elijah-Elisha stories. Yeshua must be sought out. His message in the synagogue of Nazareth was more than a hint of his high identity and status. People then were not ready to hear it, that this local son was the deliverer of the world, the source of life and freedom, the unexpected Messiah.

Chapter 3

The Heralding Yeshua
Mark 1:16-45

Some people have not yet grasped that stories are more than simply accounts of what happened. Stories are told by a storyteller to invoke meaning. Even when a storyteller attempts to be "neutral or objective," inevitably the selection of detail, the order of the story, the way it is framed with an introduction and conclusion, and many other details of the craft of story suggest morals, meanings, and symbolic import to the account.

A well-known New Testament scholar discovered that the stories of Yeshua in the four gospels present some rather different ideas about Yeshua's aims and significance (Ehrman, *Jesus, Interrupted*). His response when seeing the varied portraits of Yeshua in the gospels was to decide that they were irreconcilably contradictory. He later gave up his faith after he encountered more problems with the idea of a good God in an evil world (as told in one of his other books, *God's Problem*).

We should not be surprised to find that stories we read of Yeshua in Matthew are Matthew's stories with the personality of Matthew embedded in them. The same, of course, goes for Mark, Luke, and John. For some people, it is vital to theorize about who the authors of these gospels were and to be as precise as possible about their times, their motives, and their connection to Yeshua's apostles. Yet even without such specific knowledge about these evangelists, as they have been called, we can hear their stories, see signs of meaning not only from the events and words in the story, but also in the way the stories are told.

What if we find a complex and overlapping series of ideas about Yeshua's aims in doing this or saying that? What if Yeshua is three-dimensional and those who portray him have a variety of ideas about why or how he did this or that? The four-fold gospel stories of Yeshua give us a rare and easy opportunity to grasp more about Yeshua than we can about most ancient personalities. These stories do not begin to exhaust his personality, motives, thoughts, and essence. No story really can for even a simple person, much less a dynamic figure like Yeshua.

What about the idea that we are reading Yeshua through the filter of Mark, Matthew, Luke, and John? Should we be concerned about distortion because the stories have quite a bit of Mark in them or a great deal of John?

I suppose it would be advantageous if we had Yeshua's own account of his life. Or, if God had given us an account dictated to the evangelists in God's own words, without any personality of the writer embedded, this would be revealing. Many people read the gospels as though we are getting God's view unmixed with the views of the disciples of Yeshua. Yet that is not how the gospels work, or other Biblical literature for that matter. If you accept the idea, as I do, that these accounts are divine, you must also agree that they are human.

Yet, even if I did not believe in the divine hand guiding the accounts of the gospels toward God's ends, I would still prefer the ancient depictions of Yeshua over modern accounts. If Mark tells me that Yeshua cast out demons and a modern writer says demons are the stuff of imagination, I am not likely to accept a sterilized Yeshua, carefully cleaned up from all traces of the supernatural.

People may debate who wrote the gospels, what their sources and connections to Yeshua may be, and so on. One thing is clear: they were much closer to his lifetime and setting than we are. Their stories, even with their own personalities and quirks embedded in them, bring me as close as possible to knowing Yeshua, far closer than a modern account derived from some ideas about how to decode ancient stories and produce "neutral" history.

Artistry in the Beginning of Mark's Account

Mark's account of Yeshua begins with a prologue (1:1) and a sort of back-story (1:2-15). The main story begins with a new section (1:16-45).

One way to add meaning to a story is to frame it, to provide at the beginning and end of units some commentary or significant theme that makes sense of what comes in the middle. Some call this *inclusio* or creating literary bookends.

Mark 1:16-45 has such bookends. A perceptive reader will notice that the story is led into with an account of proclamation (1:15) and ends with another story of proclamation (1:45). You would hardly connect the two if Mark did not make the connection so obvious. In the lead-in to the story, we have a summary of Yeshua entering Galilee with a proclamation that the time of God's kingdom is near. In the concluding line of the story, we have a healed leper spreading the news all over that a healer has come and something is happening in God's timetable.

We could confidently expect, having noticed this, that this first section of Mark is going to be about the arrival of the time of God's kingdom. To understand what kingdom might have meant to Yeshua's hearers and Mark's audience at least a generation later, would be to go off to the sources of the Judaisms (plural, yes) of the time. That will mean journeying back to the Hebrew scriptures and to writings from shortly before and during the time of Yeshua and Mark.

Yet, without even leaving the story in Mark, there is much that we could notice. If a story begins and ends with a notice of the arrival of God's kingdom and large movements in the timetable of God, we might expect what comes in between those bookends to have something to do with these issues.

So, what do we have in Mark 1:16-45? We have:

- the sudden calling of disciples with a purpose of catching people (1:16-20)

- the teaching and authority over demons demonstrated by Yeshua in Capernaum (1:21-28)

- the healing in Simon Peter's house with Yeshua growing in fame and Yeshua silencing the demons from proclaiming his full identity (1:29-34)

- Yeshua seeking solitude to pray and announcing his plan to travel and proclaim (1:35-39)

- and, finally, the healing of a leper which leads to Yeshua's reputation spreading farther and wider than before (1:40-45).

Three themes emerge in this section and they might all be seen in relation to the idea of a turning over of the epochs and the coming of the kingdom of God: (1) the casting out of demons, (2) the healing of people with disease and infirmity, and (3) the tension between secrecy and spreading the fame of Yeshua far and wide.

Each of these themes deserves its own sketch, so I will save a more detailed account of them for chapters to come. Yeshua the exorcist, Yeshua the healer, and Yeshua's messianic secret are all intriguing aspects of the life and essence of this prophet, healer, and Messiah. For now, we should investigate the bookends with which Mark wraps this first section of his story. What is the significance of proclaiming the changing of times and the coming of the era of the kingdom? What does Yeshua's healing, exorcising, and desire to keep it all secret have to do with the kingdom?

Proclaiming the Kingdom

Mark's framing of this section suggests that there is something here about proclaiming the kingdom of God. How do these stories show us something about proclaiming the kingdom?

The first part of the story is about Yeshua calling disciples. It is important to note that Mark leaves out parts of the story that come before. The gospel of John tells us about incidents between Yeshua and some disciples that came before (John 1:35-51). What comes before Yeshua's call to the fishermen on the lake of Galilee does not matter to Mark for the purpose of his account. What matters here is the urgency of the mission Yeshua calls them to and the idea of catching people instead of fish. Since the story is framed with the idea of proclaiming the kingdom, it is fair to assume that the disciples are to catch men by joining Yeshua in proclaiming.

The second part of the story is about Yeshua's authority: in his teaching and over demonic powers. Mark does not specify what there is about Yeshua's teaching that causes people to wonder at his authority. For this account, it is enough to know that Yeshua's speaking evokes amazement. Yeshua is a dynamic force arriving on the scene with power and causing a stir. The encounter with the demon-possessed person reveals a secret identity of Yeshua as the Holy One of God. Yet Yeshua does not own up to this title or proclaim it himself. He commands the demon to silence, the beginning of a theme we will search out in chapter 6, the messianic secret. Yeshua's fame spreads, which is another way of saying the proclamation is happening and it is proclamation about the words and deeds of Yeshua.

The third part of the story is about healing and more exorcism of demons. Yeshua can touch someone and make their illness leave. The people of Capernaum bring many who have demons or illnesses and Yeshua heals and delivers them all. Yet, again, he commands the demons to silence. Based on the earlier account, it seems what he does not want them to spread is his secret identity as something more than simply a man.

The fourth part of the story is about Yeshua getting away from the crowds to pray in solitude and then announcing to his disciples a journey to proclaim throughout Galilee. The need for Yeshua to pray in solitude is not explained, but suggests possibly Yeshua's need for solitude to recover from public pressures and possibly a relationship with God that is secret, not for others to look on and see. The disciples then journey with Yeshua as he teaches in synagogues and casts out demons.

Finally, the last part is about a leper (a person with a skin disease that we would not call leprosy today) who begs for healing. Yeshua commands two things: that the man follow the proper procedures in Torah by going to a priest to be declared clean and that the man keep the healing miracle a secret. Yeshua does not lightly request these things, but "sternly charges" him. Yet the man does not listen and tells the story broadly with the result that Yeshua is known to all Galilee as a healer. He had to remain in the fields and countryside after that, as the crowds wanting to see him grew too large.

Yet the ending of the section returns to the summary that came right before it. Yeshua began the section proclaiming the nearness of the kingdom age and the section ends with more proclamation. The irony is that the proclamation is by someone warned sternly not to do it.

Yet something should occur to us as we read this. The proclamation by Yeshua in Mark 1:15 and by the leper in 1:45 are connected in some way. Yeshua's message had been, "the kingdom of God is near." The leper's message is, "This man healed me of leprosy." There is a connection between Yeshua's healings, exorcisms, and the kingdom. That connection will occupy us for several chapters, but we can begin to explore it here.

A Kingdom of Wellness and Liberation

It takes many stories to begin to understand Yeshua. Already this section of stories, brief as it is, requires us to investigate more closely Yeshua the exorcist, Yeshua the healer, and the messianic secret. One small collection of stories leads us off to chase down three other kinds of stories. Yet as the stories multiply and overlap, the picture of Yeshua becomes more clear.

At this early part of our searching out and sketching the essence of Yeshua, his aims, his personality, we can simply say that the kingdom of God, a Jewish idea from centuries of Jewish scriptures as well as post-Biblical writings, has something to do with wellness and liberation. We can bet that it is no coincidence that Mark places stories about exorcism and healing between the bookmarks of kingdom proclamation.

Yet we can also think forward to the rest of Yeshua's story. It is apparent that Yeshua did not actually do something which brought about a drastic change in the world. Suffering did not end with Yeshua. The demonic powers, regardless of our understanding of them, have not given up their influence on the sad story of humanity.

So, we can already see there is some sort of tension building in these stories of Yeshua. He said the kingdom was near. He did things which we might call signs of the kingdom or foreshadowings. In some ways, a little of the kingdom came with Yeshua. In some way, Yeshua was acting out a truth he believed in and hopefully we believe in too. Yet these signs Yeshua showed us are about something that has not happened in full.

Some say that Yeshua believed in a turning of the ages that never came and perhaps never will. Yeshua is a failed prophet of the apocalypse, an idealist who thought the last days were coming in his lifetime, to some of his interpreters. Others suggest that Yeshua hinted at a delay in the coming of the kingdom and that he has been misinterpreted by skeptics. What we believe about such things will depend on how we interpret the rest of the story.

Yet here at the beginning, it is good to understand the enthusiasm of the crowds, the strange willingness of disciples to leave all and follow this man, and the secret identity which he commanded demons to keep to themselves. There was something about Yeshua that brought thousands out on green hillsides in Galilee. He roused the ire of the corrupt leadership of Israel enough to be tried and convicted as a false Messiah. He was dangerous enough in the eyes of mighty Rome to be crucified. And the trouble started here, in Galilee, just forty years before a terrible war between Rome and the Jewish people. Is kingdom too strong a word to describe the point of Yeshua's teaching and his actions? But what sort of kingdom? And what does it have to do with demonic powers, with infirmities and illnesses, and why would Yeshua want to keep his identity secret?

Chapter 4

Yeshua as Exorcist
Mark 1:23-28; Luke 11:19-20; 13:32

Sometimes Yeshua said things that were not remotely comprehensible at the time. Consider, for example, the occasion when Yeshua heard that the followers of Herod Antipas wanted to kill him. He sent back a baffling message, "Look, I am casting out demons and performing healings today and tomorrow, and on the third day I will complete my work" (Luke 13:32).

The saying was nonsensical at the time Yeshua said it. Only after the resurrection could anyone make heads or tails of it. Yeshua's words suggest a progression: on days one and two he works against demonic powers and death. But the goal or completion of his work will come on day three, the day we now know to be his resurrection. In other words, in the days before his death, Yeshua was battling cosmic powers one by one, but in his resurrection he would claim a total victory.

The stories of conflict between Yeshua and the demonic powers are a sign of his greater work. From individual healings and exorcisms to the defeat of death through his own resurrection, Yeshua is at war with evil. Nowhere in the Hebrew Bible before Yeshua nor in the church writings after Yeshua do we see such a concentration of exorcisms and demonic appearances. How do we explain the frequency of demon stories in the gospels and what do they mean?

Demons in Second Temple Judaism

The formative story for most writing about demons is in Genesis 6:1-4. The sons of God cohabited with daughters of men.

The Judaism of Yeshua's day without a doubt interpreted sons of God to mean angelic beings, supernatural beings in the heavens with a nature almost divine when experienced by humans.

1 Enoch chapters 6-11 speak at length about the offspring of angels and humans, referring to them as the Watchers. These offspring of fallen angels remained on earth, always seeking out new bodies. Other traditions suggest not only the offspring, but also the fallen angels themselves resided on earth.

Numerous texts from the time dealt with angels and demons. A number of stories about exorcists were told as well. The exorcist par excellence in these traditions was Solomon, as for example in the writings of Josephus as well as in the *Testament of Solomon*. Josephus tells us in *Antiquities 8:44-45* that King Solomon had learned how to cast out demons using secret roots and herbs along with incantations or spells. He then tells a story about Eleazar, a healer and exorcist who once even performed for the emperor Vespasian. Eleazar used a root known from secret writings of Solomon to draw demons out through the nose. In his stage demonstrations he would have the demon spill a glass of water as it exited the person. It seems Eleazar was more magician and showman than a true healer.

In the book of *Tobit*, included in the Apocrypha and written about two centuries before Yeshua, the hero of the story tries to help a woman with an evil spirit who has slain seven husbands in a row in her demonic madness. The angel Raphael, who becomes in many stories the angel in charge of healing the damage done to the world by fallen angels, tells Tobit how to cast the demon out of this woman. He is to burn a fish liver and heart along with incense and the smell will drive the demon away. Raphael will then be able to imprison the demon once Tobit extracts it from the woman.

Geza Vermes says that in many stories from the period, it was knowing the "science of angels" which enabled people to overcome demons (*Jesus the Jew*, 62).

There were precursors in the Hebrew Bible for this sort of thought. Evil was preexistent in the Garden story of Genesis 3, though the story of how the serpent came to be God's enemy is left untold. The Genesis 6 story about the sons of God cohabiting with daughters of men also informs Second Temple demonology. In a number of stories, such as the Passover, God uses destructive beings and evils spirits to do his will, including such things as tormenting King Saul. The Satan or the Accuser shows up in Job and Zechariah, apparently one of the angelic court in heaven who seeks to prosecute the righteous and in so doing oppose God. Finally, in Daniel, there are spectacular battles on earth which mirror fights between angelic forces of good and evil, such as Michael versus the Prince of Persia.

Yet in all of this, from the Hebrew Bible to the later Jewish writings, there was nothing quite like the exorcism stories of Yeshua. There was never such a frequency of demons revealing themselves or of people being set free. There was never an exorcist who worked like Yeshua either, without using incantations, secret herbs, ritual objects, or even prayer.

A Synagogue Exorcism

The first story in Mark about an exorcism is a good prototype for the others. The story is simple and it establishes a pattern which many of the other stories follow in part or in whole. A man in the synagogue at Capernaum has an unclean spirit. The man (or the spirit) challenges Yeshua's authority, "Leave us alone, Yeshua the Nazarene! Have you come to destroy us? I know who you are—the Holy One of God!" (Mark 1:24). Yeshua commands silence and that the demon leave the man. The unclean spirit leaves with some turmoil, causing the man to cry out and convulse. The people are amazed and speak about the unusual authority of Yeshua's words.

There is a pattern here: (1) the demon speaks out, (2) the demon seeks to resist Yeshua's authority, (3) the demon reveals something of Yeshua's identity, (4) Yeshua commands silence, (5) Yeshua commands that the demon leave, (6) the demon seeks to harm the person while leaving, (7) onlookers are amazed (Collins, 168).

Usually, in other Jewish stories of exorcism, such as those in *Testament of Solomon*, the exorcist speaks first and asks the demon's name (Collins, 168). There is something about knowing the name or true identity of another that aids in gaining control. Yet knowing Yeshua's identity does not help any of the demons in the gospels.

The spirit is called unclean, probably referring the reader back to other ideas in the Jewish stories, such as the origin of demons in Genesis 6. Yeshua is the one who makes things clean, whole, and well. He heals leprosy (skin disease) and renders people clean, so likewise he removes unclean spirits.

The people remark about Yeshua's authority in two ways. First, his teaching is not like that of the scribes. Yeshua teaches with a different kind of authority, proceeding directly from himself. Second, even demons hear his words and must obey.

And the demons have knowledge beyond the capacity of humans. They know things from the heavens. They may not completely grasp who Yeshua is, or they would not waste their time resisting him, but they grasp more than the people around Yeshua. They know he is the Holy One of God and many other titles which they declare throughout the gospels and which Yeshua suppresses.

More Stories and Themes

Mark tells more stories about Yeshua and demons. Some are just summaries. In Mark 1:34 and 39, we simply read that Yeshua cast out many demons. In Mark 3:11, we read that many demons bowed to Yeshua and called him the Son of God. In 3:12 we find that each time Yeshua orders them not to reveal his identity, a theme which we will take up in chapter 6 about the messianic secret.

In Mark 3:20-30, Yeshua returns to his hometown and is surrounded by crowds. His family tries to pull him aside and think he is out of his mind. Some Pharisees are there and they say Yeshua uses the power of Beelzebul to cast out demons. Yeshua gives them two rational arguments and a warning. He asks why Satan would oppose himself? He also says that when defeating a power, one must first disable the leader. In these two arguments, Yeshua is saying that his work opposes and defeats Satan. He then warns these Pharisees that seeing God's power directly, the work of the Spirit, and calling it evil, is an unforgivable sin.

Mark 5 tells us of a man who lives in tombs, places unclean in Jewish thinking, somewhere on the eastern side of the lake of Galilee. The locals used to chain him, fearing his unnatural strength and terrifying insanity. But no one can restrain him anymore. He cuts and bruises himself and is more fearful than the tombs themselves.

When Yeshua comes into the area, the man runs from far off to bow before him. The demons inside refer to Yeshua as "Son of the Most High God" and beg not to be tormented. These demons are a legion, which means a unit of six Roman cohorts, numbering about 6,000 soldiers. The story has hints of Yeshua battling the spiritual powers behind Roman oppression and might.

Why is this man in the tombs? Does his own insanity lead him here, a preoccupation with death and darkness? Or did the demonic powers prefer such places? Or is it simply that tombs are an available shelter for a homeless outcast?

Legion asks to be allowed to enter a massive herd of swine and Yeshua grants that request. The swine are frightened and run into the lake and drown. Is this story about Yeshua outsmarting the demons? They asked to remain in the region and to inhabit at least some kind of body. Does Yeshua know the demons will drown themselves? Is it a symbolic victory, with the sea representing chaos and abyss, the proper abode of evil forces?

This is one of the most enigmatic stories in all of the gospels. Yet we see Yeshua as the ultimate strong man and as one who terrifies the locals more so than drawing them to God. And the only one who is not terrified is the man set free. He not only is drawn to Yeshua, but asks to travel with him and serve him. Perhaps we are to see here how those who do not understand Yeshua's identity may encounter him as a terrible power while those set free by him will want to follow him. The freed demoniac travels throughout the region of Roman cities called the Decapolis proclaiming his story.

In Mark 7, Yeshua frees the daughter of a Gentile woman from an unclean spirit. This story breaks new ground in that Yeshua is not even present at the scene when the demon leaves. The woman comes home and finds her daughter freed by the word of Yeshua from a distance.

The theme of Yeshua's power over the evil forces reaches its climax in Mark 9. The disciples, who have been successful on other occasions (Mark 6:13), have been unable to cast out a particular demon. Yeshua commands the demon and it leaves. Afterwards the disciples ask why they were unsuccessful. Yeshua's answer is part of the theme of his secret identity, running throughout Mark's telling of the story. Yeshua answers, "This kind can come out only by prayer" (Mark 9:29).

If this is true, that some demons are so powerful they can only come out by prayer, what are we to think? Yeshua did not pray. He simply commanded and the demon came out. What sort of man can do in his own authority what only prayer can do otherwise?

Authority, Evil Powers, and Kingdom

Yeshua said he cast out demons "by the finger of God" (Luke11:20), the same description used of God's power working through Moses (Exod 8:19; 31:18). He also said that today and tomorrow there would be healings and exorcisms, but on the third day he would complete his work (Luke 13:32).

Some Jewish writings from the time associated the work of Messiah with exorcism. *The Testament of Zebulon* says, "He will liberate every captive of the sons of men from Beliar" (9:8). *The Testament of Moses* said of the time of God's kingdom, "The devil will have his end" (10:1).

Yeshua's work of freeing people from demonic powers fits with the mission he stated for himself in Luke 4:18, to "proclaim release to the captives" and "set free those who are oppressed."

Yeshua claimed that the kingdom of God was near, the days of Messiah, the age of healing and restoration. In a strange way, wherever Yeshua went, death was reversed, illness healed, and demons sent away. The whole land and the whole world did not experience the change of eras and enter into the rule of God on earth. But partial and preliminary signs followed Yeshua wherever he went.

The victories over demons in Yeshua's work were signs of something greater. They were for the first and second day. But on the third, which is to say at his resurrection, he would reach his goal. The resurrection of Yeshua on the third day is the ultimate demonstration of the Age to Come, when we will be resurrected and dwell with God forever. Casting out demons was a sign along the way.

Chapter 5

Yeshua as Healer
Mark 5:21-43; Luke 7:22; 10:18.

The stories of Yeshua as healer can easily fail to impress us, either out of unbelief that such miracles could happen or out of a lack of empathy with the nameless, faceless people whose limbs, eyes, ears, and spirits were restored. A visit to the halls of a modern hospital, a loved one in the pains of illness, or a personal encounter with sickness or injury unto death can change our perspective. Where is that healer now, when we could especially use him? What difference would it make if he entered our lives or the lives of friends at their point of need and reversed hopelessness?

Yeshua was most sought out by crowds, especially in Galilee, because he brought a kind of healing they had never seen before. In the gospel of Mark we find an emphasis on these healings. Not only are there a variety of specific stories, but there are also summary statements indicating that many, whose stories we don't know, were healed by Yeshua and his disciples:

- So he healed many who were sick with various diseases and drove out many demons (Mark 1:34).

- They cast out many demons and anointed many sick people with oil and healed them (Mark 6:13).

- And wherever he would go—into villages, towns, or countryside—they would place the sick in the marketplaces, and would ask him if they could just touch the edge of his cloak, and all who touched it were healed (Mark 6:56).

Yeshua emptied the hospital halls, as it were. Entire villages saw their sick and disabled restored to full vigor and function.

Two Stories Intertwined

Mark weaves together artfully two stories, that of a synagogue ruler and a lone woman. Their combination suggests not merely that these incidents happened in combination, but something more—that perhaps the two stories are related and show something together more than they would separately. The solitary, lonely individuals are not the only ones who need hope and light from beyond, but even the structures and leaders of religious life require an infusion of saving and healing.

Yeshua has just returned from the eastern side of the Lake of Galilee. A man named Jairus approaches him, a man who presided over the synagogue in or near Capernaum. Crowds surround Yeshua, looking for healing for themselves, for others, or just to see a wonder from God and to have their faith strengthened.

Jairus is in great need, his daughter dying on a sickbed a short journey away, and falls at Yeshua's feet. The significance of a synagogue ruler kneeling at the feet of Yeshua should not be lost on us. This was no doubt an important image for those in Mark's time, when the synagogues were in conflict with the Yeshua-communities. Meanwhile, Jairus pays homage to Yeshua because he believes fully that Yeshua is the only hope for his daughter. The synagogue has come to the prophet and it is clear that greater authority is with the prophet.

As Yeshua walks beside this desperate friend, a crowd presses around him. One in the crowd has a story of private pain and loss. Her menstruation has not been right for twelve years and she suffers from excessive bleeding. She has tried the medicine of the time, spending all her money. She needs something that transcends all earthly powers, an in-breaking of divine presence. She believes that in Yeshua she can get what no one else can give her.

Due to fear or intimidation, she thinks to touch Yeshua's garment in secret. As soon as she does, with not even a word from Yeshua or a deliberate attempt on his part to heal, the woman is immediately saved from her condition. She is saved from her disease. The word for save and heal are one and the same, a fact not lost on Mark as he tells the story.

Yeshua knows that power has gone out, an expression which must remain mysterious to us. Who knows how the glory of divinity worked through the man Yeshua? In reading the story we might be tempted to maintain one of two interpretations. In one of them, Yeshua is omniscient and knows exactly who touched him and why. He asks who touched him for her benefit and not for the sake of his own need to know. In the other, Yeshua is limited in knowledge—a fact explicable from many viewpoints, even by those who are persuaded of Yeshua's divinity.

The story as we receive it is not about resolving all such mysteries, but revealing something more important. The woman is challenged by Yeshua's question. What she has done in secret she must make known. Like the synagogue ruler, she falls down before Yeshua. And though it is true that people would likewise show homage to kings and other kinds of leaders, we might be justified in seeing here early forms of Yeshua worship.

Yeshua's response again has the word that means both healing and salvation. Her faith has saved her. She can go in peace, in wholeness.

After this, Yeshua approaches Jairus' house. The mourners are there to tell him the girl is dead and there is no need for the healer. Can even Yeshua reverse death? Demons and illnesses yield before him, but death, surely that is final.

Yeshua's response, much like his response to the woman, seems to be about more than merely the healing at hand. "Don't fear; just believe," is a message which can be taken in the larger sense. It's a word to all of us and not just to Jairus on the road to Capernaum. There is comfort in our trials if the kingdom of God which Yeshua proclaimed is truly coming. Faith will help us.

Yeshua's next action invites ridicule and even anger. He tells them the girl is merely sleeping. They are too used to the normal way of working in this present age, where death wins over life, to have faith in the coming age and its powers. They see no way past the separation and loss that is our regular experience. Again we face a mystery. Was Yeshua indicating she still lived though she appeared to be dead? Or was she sleeping because death is never permanent when God's kingdom is arriving?

Yeshua enters with only his closest disciples. As the end of the story shows, this occurrence of divine power was not a display for all to see. Taking the girl's hand, Yeshua speaks to her, which Mark records in both Aramaic and Greek. The words are not an incantation or even a prayer, but simply a command to be raised.

As Yeshua raises the revived girl in the presence of her mother and father and his closest disciples, all of them are amazed. Something outside of the norm has happened here. Separation and loss have been reversed. Mourners are comforted. Faith results in a salvation. Yet, as in many other cases, Yeshua commands them to keep silent.

The Purpose of Healings

It might appear as if the healings Yeshua performed were about validating his claims to exalted status and identity. How strange, then, that Yeshua so often commanded those healed and those who witnessed not to tell anyone. If the healings were not to spread Yeshua's fame and glory all over the hills of Galilee, then what were they for?

Yeshua's healings were a liberation from the curse, a reversal of the power of Satan. The healing act itself was important. A victory over evil was won each time a person was restored.

On another occasion, Luke records the disciples, amazed that they have been able to wield divine powers like Yeshua to expel demons. Yeshua said to them, "I saw Satan fall like lightning from heaven" (Luke 10:18). These miracles were not simply signs, but acts of war against powers and oppressors that are unseen.

Yeshua's healings brought about a partial in-breaking of the kingdom of God. In another story he explained this to John, who wondered if Yeshua was the one sent from God to liberate Israel and bring about a new age. Yeshua's response was, "Go tell John what you have seen and heard: The blind see, the lame walk, lepers are cleansed, the deaf hear, the dead are raised, the poor have good news proclaimed to them" (Luke 7:22). The promises of Isaiah 35 and 61 were being realized: the lame leaping like deer, mute tongues shouting for joy, and good news being proclaimed to the poor.

It was important to Yeshua in all these stories that people believe. Your faith has saved you, he would say. Don't fear; only believe. What were they to believe?

If they listened to Yeshua's teaching, the healings were not the object of faith, but a road sign along the way. The message was about a coming kingdom and a way of being. The future hope of a time when God rules the earth, when joy and peace replace fear and sadness, is as real to Yeshua as anything in human experience. Yeshua's message, in the healings and in all other aspects of his work, is to believe with confidence in the coming kingdom of God. And for those who believe with perfect faith, this means living, to some extent, as if it has already arrived. If people will be comforted then, we should comfort them now. If only goodness will be active then, we should live by pure goodness now.

The idea of healing and saving are interwoven. Yeshua healed people and in so doing saved them. The Bible does not use the words of salvation in the sense of afterlife. Salvation is not merely some future promise to wait for while we are oppressed without hope here. Salvation is body and soul, now and also to come. We need saving from many things, the curse which manifests itself in illness, death, oppression, and despair.

The woman's story shows that something more is needed than what we can usually attain here and now. A divine presence or impartation is needed, something that will lift our experience beyond the norm and remove the malediction of evil. She had sought all this world has to offer and found nothing, but the merest touch of Yeshua's garment immediately saved her.

The synagogue ruler's story reveals that it is not only doctors that are insufficient for the task, but even the institutions of prayer and faith are not in themselves the answer. Synagogue communities, learning, and prayers are pointers along the way, not destinations.

By Mark's time there was conflict and Yeshua-followers were often unwelcome in synagogues (it probably varied from place to place). The story of Jairus is an ideal message for his time. It shows that the synagogue and Yeshua can go together, that a leader in a Galilean synagogue can kneel at Yeshua's feet and see death reversed. There is no need for conflict.

Further, it shows something else, that synagogues and churches, as right as they are in the traditions and prayers, cannot be content. Just as everywhere else, in the synagogue and church communities an in-breaking of divine presence is needed. The coming salvation and healing of the world is greatly to be desired as prayer and faith carry us along the way. Yeshua the healer operated within the synagogue structure and brought something that transcends it. He enacted the messianic age and wherever he was the kingdom blessings were present.

Chapter 6

The Messianic Secret
Mark 8:22-35

The gospels are short as biographical writings go. In such short narratives we might expect a simple story, describing what happened in Yeshua's life, what his mission was, how he was received, and the meaning of his death and resurrection. In many ways the gospels challenge us with their show-don't-tell methodology, with their deliberate ambiguity, and with their lack of overt statements defining a program or agenda.

It appears that the complexity of the gospels is due to two things. One is the complexity of Yeshua. Often he did not speak plainly, but challenged his listeners with ambiguous and onerous sayings. The power of his speaking lay in the authority with which he spoke and also in the nearly impenetrable and unanticipated direction of his answers. The other is the apparent decision, by the evangelists, to present Yeshua much as he was and not to greatly simplify. Of course, they did some explaining and clarifying, yet for the most part they depict Yeshua as a challenging personality, a goad to wisdom, a demanding intellect. This is, further, a sign that they are largely presenting early, traditional material which has not been dramatically theologized. This not to say that shaping and agendas are completely absent, but they are muted, understated.

Many readers are disappointed that Yeshua did not simply state his identity as Messiah and Lord. Equally they are dismayed that Yeshua did not render and clear and easily memorable guide to spirituality or inheritance of eternal life.

In fact, Yeshua is known for another theme in his deeds and sayings, a secretive theme. He told his disciples once than he spoke in parables so that only a few would understand (Mark 4:11). He repeatedly silenced unclean spirits who had access to higher planes of knowledge and were aware of his identity (Mark 1:25). He commanded those who witnessed healings and resurrections not to tell anyone (Mark 5:43). He downplayed talk of his status. He fled from crowds eager to make him king (John 6:15). He was sometimes evasive when directly questioned at his trial about his royal identity (Mark 15:2).

This is not to say that Yeshua did not own up, repeatedly, to lofty expressions of his identity and purpose. Yet he generally chose expressions off the beaten path, describing his authority in unusual ways or his status as the crux of salvation in unusual metaphors. He left his hearers confused, even his closest disciples. The church has not come to unanimous agreement either, through all the centuries, about the details of Yeshua's message and the meaning of his deeds.

Yet for all this ambiguity and obscurity, Yeshua fascinates and draws followers rather than simply repelling them with an insurmountable challenge. His disciples, for example, were committed to a very high level of following him even though they did not understand what he was about until after the resurrection. One story in particular brings the theme of the messianic secret to its high point and develops the theme of misunderstanding, true identity, and the need for a sober mind and clear vision.

Walking Trees and Suffering Messiahs

On more than one occasion, Yeshua healed without a word or even without a touch. People did not need even to be in Yeshua's presence to be healed. Yet on a few other occasions, Yeshua engaged in some kind of physical ceremony, sometimes appearing magical. In Mark 8, in Bethsaida near Yeshua's usual base in Capernaum, he healed a blind man after spitting on his eyes. The possible reason for this physical act in combination with the healing may become evident as the story continues.

There are other unusual aspects to this blind man of Bethsaida's healing. Yeshua led him away to a private place, away from the village (Collins, 393). The disciples apparently were with Yeshua outside of the village and witnessed the healing. This is apparent because in Mark 8:27, Yeshua continued on from there with his disciples.

Why would Yeshua draw a man to a private place with only his disciples to witness the healing? We might guess that something Yeshua is doing is for their benefit. We might also surmise that they understood the message, if not right away, later. Mark understood and kept the story of the blind man of Bethsaida adjacent to the story of Caesarea Philippi. The stories go together and form a lesson about Yeshua's identity.

After spitting on his eyes, Yeshua asked what the blind man could see. His vision was restored but not completely. He saw, but with distortion. The same would be true of the disciples and Yeshua would shortly reveal to them what was distorted about their understanding.

After a journey, in a place of pagan worship which was an inspiring spectacle and still is, Yeshua asked his disciples about his identity. He asked, in effect, "You who have journeyed with me, who do people think I am, and is your understanding of higher quality than theirs?"

The disciples could easily see that people were amazed by Yeshua's miracles and the authority of his teaching and speaking as a voice for God. In the memory of the people, Yeshua was a figure like Elijah. God worked through him as through no one else. His words were the words of God's trusted messenger. It was plain for all to see—except those who believed Yeshua to be a sorcerer in league with demons or a trickster of some sort.

In the recent memory of the people, another who was like Elijah had appeared. Some thought of Yeshua, no doubt, as the Elisha to John the Baptist's Elijah. The spirit and power that had rested on John must have come upon Yeshua (see 1 Kgs 19:16, 19). And just as Elisha exceeded his master in wonders and deeds (2 Kgs 2:9), so Yeshua was exceeding John.

But Yeshua was not satisfied with these answers. He expected his own disciples to know more. "Who do you say that I am?" he asked directly. Peter answered that Yeshua was more than Elijah. He was Messiah. In Matthew's version, he said not only Messiah, but also Son of the Living God. To an Israelite the title Son of God was synonymous with Messiah, since David was called God's son (2 Sam 7:14; Psa 2:7).

The disciples had insider knowledge. They knew Yeshua as more than a wonder worker, as more than a prophet.

Yet their knowledge was distorted also. Yeshua was about to prove it to them.

He proceeded to mix up categories in their minds, to challenge their certainty and expand their thinking. The Son of Man, Yeshua said, referring to the figure of heavenly authority to whom the kingdom is given in Daniel 7, will suffer many things.

Peter was overcome. Who knows what he was thinking as he took on his master and teacher? Mark says Peter rebuked him. The student was ready to tell the teacher how it is. The Son of Man does not suffer. He rules. It was time to put this talk of suffering away and get on with the mission they were most eager to see.

The meaning of the messianic secret theme and of the blind man of Bethsaida's healing is beginning to unfold.

Titles such as Messiah, Son of God, and Son of Man communicated to Yeshua's generation a conquering king. It awoke in them the great desire of the Israelites in the first century, that the oppression of Rome would be answered with divine force or at least a divinely led rebellion as in the days of the Maccabees. Many apocalyptic writings of the time contained such speculations. The words of Daniel easily suggested it. The time seemed as right as ever and if anything God's appearance seemed overdue.

It often seems clear to mortals what God should do.

Yeshua turned back Peter's rebuke with a stunning counter: you are speaking for Satan and not for God. You, my close disciple and friend, are speaking diabolical words, which will work great evil and prevent a greater good. Let God be God and wait for him.

If Yeshua's closest disciples were so colored by popular expectations, how could the masses or the teachers and leaders of Israel understand? Yeshua was all the things these friends wanted him to be but nothing would happen the way these friends expected. Perhaps we can understand it this way: redemption does not come through violence. Violence will come at the day of judgment, but now is not that time.

And many of those who desire violence on God's enemies do not realize their own need for redemption. Like the blind man of Bethsaida, when he was half-healed, we too easily see a distorted picture of ourselves and the world. Yeshua's mission was something deeper than annihilation of enemies.

Yeshua's mission, as seen in many of his sayings and deeds, is about reordering the expected, transforming the present so it resembles the future time of glory.

Messianic Secret as Denial?

Some have supposed that all the secrecy, the parables, the silencing of those who would proclaim Yeshua's true identity, was because Yeshua did not own up to that identity. Yeshua did not accept the idea that he was Messiah or Lord or Son of God. In this school of thinking, Yeshua's preferred title, Son of Man, meant simply human, as in the book of Ezekiel.

It is only possible to arrive at this conclusion by a very selective approach. Either the many sayings in which Yeshua expressed an exalted identity are not genuine to Yeshua or they must all be interpreted so as not to be an affirmation of exalted status.

E.P. Sanders, for example, is very cautious, to the point of dismissing evidence that Yeshua believed himself to have exalted status. In his book *The Historical Figure of Jesus*, Sanders tends to the side of caution or even dismissal in accepting evidence for Yeshua's own view of his role. He says, for example, that Yeshua did not accept the title Messiah as the best definition of his identity (p. 242). Messiah was the preferred title of the followers of Yeshua in the generations after him and so the title stuck, but with no encouragement from Yeshua himself. As for the title, Son of Man, Sanders suggests it is not clear that Yeshua used it in the exalted sense except in a few cases, and in those cases he may have meant someone other than himself who was to come later (pp. 247-8). Yet Sanders does admit that the evidence is overwhelming that Yeshua saw his status as exalted and that king or viceroy of God's kingship might be better ways of viewing Yeshua's self-understanding (p. 248).

It is important for us to consider Yeshua's self-understanding. There are dozens of stories to be explored to draw in closer to that elusive idea which Yeshua had of his own role in God's plan.

Yet, in this story, this defining story of the messianic secret theme, we can at least address one of the points Sanders raises. Does Yeshua deny being the Messiah in Mark 8? Or is it more accurate to say that Yeshua redirects messianic expectations in Mark 8?

Sanders says that Yeshua's followers, after his time, chose Messiah as the best label for Yeshua's identity and redefined or narrowly defined what the title Messiah is all about (p. 243). Yet it would seem that redefinition or more precise definition of the role of Messiah was not something that waited for Yeshua's followers. Yeshua himself taught to his inner circle a more defined idea of Messiah.

The Son of Man must suffer many things. Too many people, like the half-healed blind man, would see Messiah with distorted vision. Yeshua's role and the clues he left of his identity and aims are both different and more exalted than the popular messianic expectations. Texts that promise future redemption and a redeemer combine in unexpected ways. Themes of suffering and serving on the one hand and exaltation, permanence, and kingship would combine through a world of inter-textual references in the allusive and elusive words of Yeshua.

The messianic secret is not impossible to grasp. In the Jewish world of ideas, both the ones we know were written before, during, and shortly after Yeshua's time and the ones written much later in rabbinic literature, a repository of texts combine in a rich world of midrashic intertextuality. Yeshua hinted at his sense of identity and mission through a world of texts from the Torah, Psalms, and prophets.

By downplaying hasty talk of his messianic mission, Yeshua bought time to educate his inner circle. Even so they would not understand (so that at his death, they had all left him and were in despair). Yet they were prepared to understand after the fact, after death would be reversed in exaltation.

Also, by downplaying popular notions of messianic identity, Yeshua bought time before the authorities decided he was too dangerous. At his trial, the leaders of Israel found it difficult to find evidence against him. They were barely able to make a case with Rome that he should be executed as a potential rebel.

The messianic secret is also a warning for those after the exaltation of Yeshua who might continue to misunderstand his mission. History has shown this warning to go sadly unheeded and that the secrecy theme in the gospels needs much more attention in popular understanding. Yeshua's followers now, as then, need what was given to the blind man: to look intently and have our sight restored.

Chapter 7

The Temple Cleansing
John 2:13-22

In perhaps the most decisive event in Yeshua's life he took on the leading institution of Jewish life and made a scene. Most historians studying the life of Yeshua are convinced the action of Yeshua in the Temple was a leading cause of his death. The authorities simply had to consider him a threat afterward.

The story is not without difficulties. In the fourth gospel, Yeshua's action in the Temple is depicted early, at least two Passovers before his death. In Matthew, Mark, and Luke, Yeshua's Temple action is depicted as one of the last things he did before he was arrested. So, as we look for the context of this action in Yeshua's life, we are confronted right away by a question: was this something he did early in his career or was it late? Was it one of many actions that identified him to the authorities as a threat or was it the decisive actions leading to his death?

The Temple cleansing story is also critical because on it hangs one of the great questions about Yeshua's aim and message: was he against the Temple in some way? Did Yeshua come to say that the old way of worshipping God on Mount Zion and offering animals and chanting Psalms was passing away? Did he come to replace Judaism with a new order, a higher spiritual worship replacing the inferior, ritual and physical ceremonies of the Jerusalem Temple?

And the story is hard to understand for another reason as well. One of the hardest things to decide, whether we read it in the synoptic gospels or in the fourth gospel, is the question: what was Yeshua angry about?

To search for answers about this event in Yeshua's life, loaded with meaning and surrounded in mysteries, we'll consider the story as told in the fourth gospel, with some reference to the synoptics. The fourth gospel definitely gives us a later version of the story. It offers a bit more explanation that the versions in Mark, Matthew, and Luke. It also offers a potential solution to a difficulty in harmonizing the life of Yeshua. How could someone who was arrested just after an action against the Temple not have witnesses at his trial who could verify that he had spoken against the Temple?

Authentic or Invented, Early or Late?

Right away the story as told in the fourth gospel is suspected by some of being inauthentic. It makes less sense, some have said, that this incident could have happened two years or more before Yeshua's death. It makes more sense, as the synoptics suggest, that this event was a life-ender for Yeshua. For some, the obvious difference in timing of this story between the fourth and the other gospels makes it hard to believe anything we read about Yeshua's life is historically based. If the keepers of the Yeshua tradition can't even get this right, why should we believe anything they say about his life?

Raymond Brown, perhaps the leading commentator on the fourth gospel, points out that arguments for the Temple cleansing as late in Yeshua's career are strong (*John I-XII*, 117-8). The chief priests in Jerusalem would have to react to such a threat to the Temple status quo. Further, it is doubtful that an action like this would come early in Yeshua's career. This action only makes sense if he was already seen by some as a prophet and had a following who would see and learn from it.

Yet Brown notes the strong arguments for the other side as well, that the Temple cleansing could have been early in Yeshua's career. It makes no sense, some have pointed out, to take at face value the synoptic timeline in which Yeshua comes to Jerusalem only once in his career, at the very end. A Torah-faithful Jew like Yeshua would have come three times a year. And the fourth gospel is more realistic in depicting Yeshua's frequent trips to Jerusalem. Furthermore, in the synoptic versions of the story, Yeshua brings up John the Baptist in his answer when challenged on what basis he is doing this in the Temple. Wouldn't a reference to John the Baptist make more sense early in Yeshua's career and not late, since by then John had been dead for some time? And at Yeshua's trial in the synoptics, no true witness could be brought having heard Yeshua say anything about the Temple being destroyed? How can this be if he had said it only days before?

Brown is ready to propose a solution which handles all of the evidence neatly and explains the difference in timing quite well. To begin with, we should note that the fourth gospel's story actually comes in two parts: the action of driving out vendors and the dispute scene with Yeshua speaking of the Temple being destroyed and rebuilt. As Brown notes, the best arguments for late concern the action itself and the best arguments for early concern the dispute in words. Brown's solution is simple: the dispute conversation between Yeshua and the Temple authorities happened early while the action of driving out the vendors happened late. The fourth gospel puts them together early, at the time the saying about destroying and rebuilding the Temple happened.

Based on this theory, then, Yeshua, early in his career, got involved in some dispute with Temple authorities that led them to question him. He responded with a curious saying about the Temple being destroyed and rebuilt in three days. Though the synoptics do not tell this story about Yeshua's saying, they bring it up at his trial and at his crucifixion. False witnesses are brought to Yeshua's trial claiming he said he would destroy the Temple. And on the cross, people mocked Yeshua saying, "If you can rebuild the Temple in three days, come down from there."

A Prophet Against the Temple?

What about the question of Yeshua's stance toward the Temple? Was he against the Temple in some way? Did he believe that some later Christian ideal of worship which would replace the Temple? Did Yeshua think that sacrifice and a house for the Presence of God was primitive or unworthy of the coming age of eternal life?

The story in the fourth gospel will not let us think this way. Yeshua calls the Temple his Father's house, hardly an expression of contempt. And he is angry that his Father's house is being abused. His concern is for its holiness, not for its demise. And when the disciples observe Yeshua's action, they think of Psalm 69, about the one like David who is consumed with zeal for God's house. The Temple cleansing is the story of one who loves the Temple, not one who despises it.

Is this consistent with the depiction of Yeshua and his relation to the Temple overall in all four gospels? The answer would have to be yes. As an adolescent, Yeshua remained at the Temple during a family trip and told his surprised parents that they should expect to find him at his Father's house. In a series of woes on the Pharisees in Matthew 23, he criticizes his opponents for failing to understand that both the Temple and the altar are holy. Yeshua's predictions about the Temple being destroyed are not an exception, but a proof of his reverence for it. With tears Yeshua describes the coming desolation, not with rejoicing.

The Source of Yeshua's Anger

If we admit that the Temple cleansing really happened and that Yeshua really spoke about the Temple destruction and rebuilding in three days, we still need to understand, what was Yeshua angry about? What caused him to fashion a whip and drive out vendors and overturn tables of coins on the Temple stones?

Adela Yarbro Collins, in her commentary on Mark, gives some of the best information (527-8). She argues that the vendors were not, as some have supposed, in the court of the gentiles, but rather in the outer court, in the royal portico. Yeshua's anger is directed at the secularization of the outer courts of the Temple, which is the fault primarily of Herod the Great.

When Herod rebuilt the Temple, he greatly enlarged the Temple platform. This might seem to add to the glory of God except for one thing. Herod built a portico and colonnades in the expanded area, which was modeled on Greek and Roman temples. These outer courts would be a public forum and a marketplace. Yeshua,

Collins suggests, was like Ezekiel and Zechariah and the writer of the Temple Scroll in insisting on the sanctity of the entire Temple platform. The idea that outer courts could be attached and function as a marketplace devalued the sanctity of the entire platform. Vendors should not be allowed on the platform of God's holy Temple.

And as for the money changers, it was not a problem that they traded coins so people could pay the Temple tax. The problem, Collins suggests, is that they used the Tyrian silver coins. These had an image of Baal Melqart on them, the Tyrian version of Heracles. These money changers were enabling a system in which people paid the holy Temple tax with pagan coinage.

This understanding of the Temple cleansing fits well with the reaction of Yeshua's disciples. They saw Yeshua as walking in the footsteps of his predecessor, David, who had written in Psalm 69, "Zeal for your house will devour me."

Double Entendres

And that is what is really interesting about the story as told in the fourth gospel. We have in this story a collection of double meanings uttered by Yeshua, sayings with hidden import only to be revealed later. And there are three of them. Two are early and one is late, according to our theory about the timing of the two parts of this story.

The first double entendre is from the late event itself, the action of driving out vendors. The disciples reacted by quoting from the Psalm about zeal for God's house consuming Yeshua. In the original context, David is saying that his passion for the worship at the sanctuary has made him an object of scorn to his enemies. So too, Yeshua is guilty of a fervor for the holiness of the house of his Father. His fervor puts him at odds with the compromises of the chief priests and the people. But there is a further meaning hidden in these words, which the fourth gospel is very aware of and presents to us, the readers. Yeshua's zeal for the Temple will consume him, devour him, lead to his arrest and crucifixion at the hands of the chief priests and the Romans.

The second and third double entendre come from the earlier event, Yeshua's dispute with Temple authorities and his saying about the Temple being destroyed and rebuilt in three days. To be exact, Yeshua said, "Destroy this temple and in three days I will raise it up again." His hearers think he means that they will in some way be responsible for destroying the Temple. And that is true, it is the verdict of the rabbis' own view of Jewish history that the leaders of the Second Temple sinned and brought the Temple destruction on from God. Yet this is not what Yeshua means in the fullest sense. He refers to his body when he speaks here of the Temple. He speaks in riddles, foretelling that these leaders will destroy the Temple of his body by handing him over to Rome.

Likewise, Yeshua does not mean that in any sense he or his disciples will rebuild the Temple building in three days. He means his own body, raised on the third day. No one could possibly understand the import of his words at the time he uttered them. But after Yeshua was raised, see vs. 22, the disciples and many others would understand.

A Prophet and Martyr With Purpose

What do we learn from the Temple cleansing story? What does it tell us about Yeshua?

First, we learn that Yeshua had a zeal for the holiness of Jerusalem, the Temple, God's presence in the Holy City. He was a prophet who called his generation to greater faithfulness to Torah, not to walk away from Torah. The Temple was, for Yeshua, his Father's house, a place too sacred to have markets directly attached to it or to use pagan coins in its offerings.

Second, we learn that Yeshua knew of his inevitable death and resurrection early, not late. As Raymond Brown has argued, Yeshua's dispute and saying about rebuilding the Temple happened early, not late. This is confirmed at the trial scenes and crucifixion scenes in the synoptics. This complex tradition, with its double entendres and its fourfold existence according to two different chronologies, is too elaborate to have been invented. The Temple cleansing and the saying about rebuilding are genuine according to realistic standards of historical scrutiny.

Yeshua's aim was to reform his generation or to die for it. His life was not about being a victim of circumstances beyond his control, but rather about following a path set out for him early and with clarity of purpose. He set his face toward Jerusalem, to love it, to show zeal for it, and to die at the hands of Jerusalem's leaders who were supposed to share the same zeal but did not.

Chapter 8

The Handwashing Dispute
Mark 7:1-23

In Mark 7 we have a story about another dispute between Yeshua and those in Israel who saw themselves as the Torah teachers of the future. In Yeshua's time, the Pharisees were a small movement and, in spite of many studies which have failed to grasp this, their influence was not yet broad over the Jewish communities in Israel or the diaspora. The days of rabbinic dominance in Judaism would not come for centuries.

No matter how we read the story in Mark 7 we're bound to run into problems. We will encounter problems of our modern context, of centuries of Christian readings, of historical understanding, of coherence, of translation, of theology, and not least of spirituality.

In terms of our modern context, we are prone to think in terms of Judaism and Christianity in recent history. We are handicapped by the pervasive idea of many centuries that Judaism and Christianity are mutually exclusive. It is all too easy to read Yeshua as the representative of Christianity which is superseding Judaism. There could also be a Jewish reading of the story, a non-messianic reading, which equally misses the point. I will attempt a reading that reflects Judaism in Yeshua's time and at the same time takes seriously his messianic claims.

A problem less often considered is that centuries of Christian readings have ignored a crucial fact of the story. Yeshua did practice ritual handwashing. We conclude this because his questioners ask why "some of his disciples" ate with unwashed hands. It seems Yeshua did not. This is one of several factors in the story that undercuts any reading which finds Jewish traditions to be contradictory to Yeshua's message.

There are problems of historical understanding. A frequent claim is that ritual handwashing was a recent innovation, representing the work of the Pharisees in expanding Temple holiness procedures into the home. Yet, as we will see, there is evidence that handwashing was more widespread and far older.

There are problems of coherence. The Pharisees advocate a practice which expands Temple holiness, bringing handwashing into the daily life of Jews. This is a practice which seeks to honor God and his holiness which is seen pervading all of life. Yet Yeshua's response is to cite Isaiah 29:13, about people honoring God only with lips and not with their hearts. How does a ritual intended to honor God become evidence of insincere devotion? Is Yeshua's argument coherent?

Largely unrecognized, there is a problem of translation. Modern English translations supply a few words in verse 19. Some supply "he declared." One even supplies "In saying this, Jesus declared." Verse 19 is taken as a comment added by Mark about what Yeshua declared. Yet the phrase says only "cleansing all foods." Is it part of Yeshua's statement, rounding off his sentence? Or is it, as has been assumed, a remark from the gospel writer?

As if these problems were not enough, the Mark 7 story raises issues of theology. In one reading, the prevalent one, Yeshua comes against a divine commandment, the commandment that Jews should not eat any meats other than those specifically allowed by Leviticus 11. Somehow, the dominant reading asserts, a dispute about ritual handwashing becomes an occasion for the Messiah to overturn a law of the Torah, a law uttered by God and written through Moses. Is the Mark 7 story justification for a low view of the Hebrew Bible, a view which is all too common in Christian history? Does this story pit Yeshua against the scriptures of Israel, dividing the Bible into its spiritual and substandard parts? Does this divide God, with the Father advocating dietary purity and the Son freeing Israel to violate the Father's commands?

Finally, we have here a problem of spirituality. What exactly does spiritual living look like to Yeshua? It seems he engaged in handwashing himself, but is he criticizing the Pharisees for doing so? Is there some inner-outer distinction being made here, so that ethics of the heart matter while actions of the body do not? How does Yeshua suggest we should honor God with our hearts as well as our lips?

Clues to a Better Reading

Reading Yeshua's life and message in the context of his own times has been a helpful corrective thus far in searching out, as best we can with our many limitations, who he was and what he was about. If we have learned anything, it should be that Yeshua represents Judaism and not Christianity. Yet, and this is an important corrective, there was no more one Judaism in Yeshua's time than there is in ours. Judaism had many streams. And Yeshua did not fit precisely into any one of them. We must keep in mind the uniqueness of Yeshua's message as we read Mark 7 in context.

It is possible to read Mark 7 as one of many stories revealing a disjunction between his own belief and practice and the later belief and practice of the Church. Is Mark reading the story incorrectly, assuming that Yeshua is critical of Jews and favorable toward Christian indifference to the Law? I will read it differently, as a criticism of a certain misplaced priority in the spiritual life of these Pharisees. The disjunction is not between later Christianity and the Judaism of Yeshua. It is a Jewish critique from one Jewish philosophy to another.

Following the commentary of Adela Yarbro Collins (pp. 345-7), I will assume that ritual handwashing was widespread in Israel and in the diaspora. In the *Letter of Aristeas*, c. 170 C.E., we read that the legendary seventy-two translators of the Septuagint washed their hands daily before prayer in the sea. This is repeated in Josephus' version of the story of the translators of the Torah into Greek. It is true that washing before prayer has a different purpose, but it shows nonetheless that handwashing was a widespread issue and not something recent and limited in scope.

As to the coherence of Yeshua's argument, we should consider that his reaction may be to a spiritual deficiency in his questioners more so than some deficiency in a tradition of handwashing. This would explain why Yeshua apparently engaged in handwashing while at the same time being critical of his questioners. Yeshua's argument is that they are guilty of insincere claims to devotion, that their practice of Torah can even at times overrule a divine commandment, and that they have not properly understood impurity. Impurity cannot be ingested with food. So their concern is imaginary, but meanwhile, they are far too little concerned with the impurity that comes out in unethical actions and attitudes.

It is possible that the translation issues are unsolvable. Those who see this as a remark made by Mark assume that the "and he said to them" in vs. 18 is the understood verb for the last phrase of vs. 19. In other words, they assume the structure of the sentence is as follows, "And he said to them, 'So and so,' thus cleansing all foods." But the sentence might better be read with "cleansing all foods" completing Yeshua's own sentence. In that case, Yeshua's point is that food passes out of the body, cleansing all foods. That is, impurity cannot be ingested since food passes through the body. This would be an argument to the effect that handwashing is not necessary. Would Yeshua participate in a ritual that he deemed unnecessary? It is possible, since the ritual could be seen as honoring God's holiness rather than a necessary means to avoid impurity.

The theological problem should be easier to resolve. The idea that Yeshua would view the institutions of the Hebrew Bible, such as Temple, sacrifice, and dietary law, as substandard or temporary is unthinkable. Even in this very story, Yeshua criticizes his opponents for making rulings that void divine commands. Yeshua uses the divine command to honor parents in his example. But how could he criticize his opponents for voiding the command to honor parents and then in the next breath himself void a divine command to restrict the diet? Furthermore, the discussion is about ritual handwashing and not whether the forbidden foods of Leviticus should become food for Yeshua's followers.

Finally, there is the problem of spirituality to consider. What course is Yeshua recommending in his teaching? What spiritual problem is he correcting? Many have assumed that Yeshua opposes rituals. This is strange since he participated in so many rituals, including, apparently, the ritual of handwashing. Is Yeshua advising his followers to be more like Sadducees, who keep only the written commands and avoid all traditional observances added to what Moses wrote? This would not fit the Yeshua we read about in the gospels. But maybe the issue Yeshua is addressing is not handwashing per se, but the misplaced priorities of his questioners. The point of Isaiah 29:13, which Yeshua quotes, is not that rituals are bad, but that people put on a show of honoring God that is not sincere. Somehow, in asking Yeshua about his disciples' failure to engage in handwashing, the Pharisees are revealing a spiritual deficiency. Their hearts are in the wrong place.

Reading the Story in Context

Some Pharisees and scribes traveled up from Judea to witness Yeshua's work and teaching. It is likely they were checking him out. He was a potential threat to their aspirations for authority in Israel as the true teachers of Torah. Also, being highly political creatures, the Pharisees may have realized Yeshua could be a troublemaker inciting tension with Rome.

While observing Yeshua and his disciples, they asked why some of his disciples did not practice handwashing before eating. We cannot know exactly how standard handwashing was for ordinary Israelites. Perhaps they assumed that since Yeshua was a teacher with a following that he would be scrupulous, as they were, about such things.

Ritual handwashing before meals was a tradition based loosely on the purity laws of the Torah. Nowhere did the Torah ever suggest that washing hands could remove impurity from the hands. Most issues of purity either required waiting until sundown or, if the impurity was more severe, possibly bathing, laundering clothes, and perhaps a longer period of time, such as seven days. Ritual handwashing was an innovation, though not recent. It's purpose, quite likely, was to keep any impurity that might have been caught in the marketplace unknowingly, from infecting the food and entering the body. Yeshua may have had his own reasons for practicing handwashing, perhaps as a ceremony honoring the holiness of God.

Yeshua's reaction to the question was immediately hostile and accusatory. With prophetic zeal, Yeshua charged them using language from Isaiah. Their question revealed a lack of insight into the ways of God. It was likely their concern for a relatively unimportant tradition that sparked Yeshua's ire. They fit well the words of Isaiah, as a people concerned more with a show of devotion than with true desire to know and follow God's ways. Their question might be compared to person who attends a powerful worship community and then asks if the lighting was improper or why people dress a certain way. Their question revealed a short-sighted priority.

While accusing them, Yeshua referred to an egregious example of misplaced piety. The example Yeshua used is likely the most extreme, perhaps an uncommon duplicity, but one which represented a general principle in which vows made for wicked reasons could have more sanctity than a divine command. Collins discusses the hypocritical use of vows as a means to prevent parents from using the property of a child (352-3). It is not necessarily the case that these Pharisees had done anything of the kind, but that their way of interpreting Torah would allow for such deceit.

After denouncing the insincerity of these would-be guardians of Torah and purity, Yeshua put forward his own principles for understanding impurity. First, he declared that no one can contract impurity by eating food. There is no case in which we need to worry that, having touched some impure object or person, that this impurity could be transmitted to the food and cause further impurity in our eating. Second, he declared that the far greater concern about impurity should involve our unethical actions and attitudes. It could be tempting to follow a kind of spirituality built on avoiding even secondary impurities. But the harder task, and one far more important, is living out godly, ethical lives.

The disciples did not understand exactly what Yeshua meant. Perhaps they needed more information about how these principles would work in practice. Perhaps those of the disciples who had washed their hands were surprised by Yeshua's teaching. The teacher did not go easier on his students than he did on his opponents. They were foolish, lacking understanding.

So Yeshua gave a logical reason to back up his claim that eating food cannot transmit impurity. The food we eat goes through the stomach and passes out of the body, cleansing all foods. By contrast, however, unethical actions and attitudes are not merely in the digestive system, but at the core of a person's being, the heart. And while food passes away, wickedness remains.

At issue in this story is the proper interpretation of Torah. Yeshua frequently engaged in illuminating true principles of righteousness from the Torah. He sought the essence of commandments to define them at the level of motivations, beliefs, consequences, and glorification of God and not self.

Understanding the groups in Yeshua's time, the Pharisees were closer to his way of seeing Torah than almost anyone else. Yeshua's corrective was not only for them, but all Israel. Yeshua's generation needed teachers to bring the true intent of the Torah to them. Yeshua's harshness with the Pharisees, but also with his disciples, represents not that these were furthest from the right way, but were those from whom he expected more.

Yeshua's interpretation, of which we learn a great deal in this passage, has nothing to do with repealing the purity laws. Ritual handwashing was not a Torah law in the first place. Rather, Yeshua desired that his generation would see in the Torah the love of God and neighbor as of highest priority.

These Pharisees and scribes were worried about unnecessary details. Yeshua wanted them to see the real problem. It wasn't whether this teacher's disciples followed this tradition or some other tradition. Rather, the Torah is about ethical actions and attitudes which promote justice, love, and mercy. God was not about to visit Israel with judgment for failing to be scrupulous with extra regulations. It was needless hatred, unseemly pride, religious hypocrisy, blindness to the work of God appearing before their eyes, and apathy about the needs of the poor and hurting that would doom Yeshua's people.

Yeshua's view of impurity within is an ethic worth living. If only we could view ourselves as unclean and in need of God's cleansing for our evil thoughts, murderous attitudes, self-indulgent desires, and unkind words, we would strive to do better. We would come to God for cleansing, which Yeshua taught would be given freely to us as long as we forgive those who wrong us as well. We would take more seriously, not less seriously, divine commands. We would have a clearer picture of our goal, to be pure and see God, to live as Yeshua lived. Following Yeshua's prescription would increase good thoughts, faithfulness, forgiveness, love for neighbor, contentment, honesty, restraint, healing words, a proper sense of our importance, and wisdom that comes from God.

Chapter 9

The Prodigal Story
Luke 15:11-32

A prophet tells stories in a prophet's words. For many readers, including some of the academicians, recognizing Yeshua's role in the long line of Israelite prophets would be a major step forward in getting his context right. Perhaps for some the concept of Messiah has so overshadowed Yeshua's role as prophet that the latter has been nearly ignored. For many readers the problem is, no doubt, a lack of intimate familiarity with the words of Israel's prophets.

The prophets of Israel told stories and used images, sometimes congenial images, but often disturbing ones. They had an unsettling effect on their audience. And they told and retold Israel's story in creative ways (as N.T. Wright emphasizes in *Jesus and the Victory of God*).

We could say the same of Yeshua. He used homey as well as discomfiting images, a bit here about the flowers in the grass and a bit there about wailing and gnashing teeth. He told and retold Israel's story, though few readers have known to look for Israel's story in Yeshua's parables. It is certainly true that in Yeshua's most beloved story, the Prodigal Son, few readers have seen Israel's story told here in an inflammatory manner.

Prophets' Tales and Yeshua's Parables

If N.T. Wright has made a solid and enduring point about the meaning of Yeshua's life and teachings, it is that Yeshua often reframes or subverts the usual tellings of Israel's story (*Jesus and the Victory of God*, see pp. 125-133). People in every age are familiar with certain stories which define their nation, their generation, or which are part of the culture in some major way. In Israel, there were stories about a covenant, an exile, a return, and a great future restoration.

On virtually every page of the gospels we find evidence that the story of Israel's past shame and future glory was profoundly on the minds of Yeshua's generation. People speak of the kingdom of God and of Elijah, they go out to John in the desert, they ask for signs, they spread out garments and branches beneath the feet of Yeshua as he enters Jerusalem. They cry out, "*Hoshiah na,*" from Psalm 118, "Please save us." The disciples ask if they can sit at Yeshua's right hand in his glory as Israel's messianic king. They ask if he is at this time going to restore the kingdom to Israel. A Pharisee cries out exuberantly, "Blessed is he who will eat bread in the kingdom of God."

Israel was thinking of the coming time of restoration. Yeshua's generation thought of itself still in exile, as N.T. Wright has emphasized in his readings in both *The New Testament and the People of God* and *Jesus and Victory of God.* Israel's national story, in outline, is simple: election and initial blessing followed by disappointing God, exile, shame, restoration, vindication, and ultimate glory.

This story of Israel is told again and again in the prophets. Moses first told it this way: God, like an eagle, found Israel in the desert, spread his wings over him, and carried him to a safe place on the heights, feeding him curds and honey from the rocks. Israel grew fat, though, and rebelled, neglecting the rock which had fed him. So God sent Israel into exile and shamed him with a people not chosen, a perverse nation. Yet God will not cast him off forever, but will vindicate his people by the end. God, who alone puts to death and gives life, calls the nations to join him in the last days as he restores Israel (Deut 32:1-43).

Isaiah sang a song of the vineyard. The beloved dug all the stones out around a hill and planted a vineyard. He planted the best vines. He built a tower to guard it. But for all his work and expectation the vineyard produced worthless grapes. The vineyard owner looked for justice, but found bloodshed. So he burned it. Israel went into exile for lack of knowledge (Isa 5:1-30). Many other parts of the story, including restoration, are told in the rest of Isaiah.

Jeremiah tells the story of Israel's shame, exchanging God for cheap idols and useless deities. God brought Israel into a fruitful land, he says, but the people defiled it. In fact, they turned the good land into an abomination. The prophets sought Baal instead of the Lord. No other nation so quickly changed its gods as Israel, carving out worthless cisterns that held no water, seeking gods who gave no profit. So God will shame Israel as they have shamed him (Jer 2:1-37). As is the case with Isaiah, this is not the end of the story. It continues to restoration, vindication, and ultimate glory many times in the pages of Jeremiah.

Ezekiel tells the story in more than one way also. The most memorable is of Israel as a rejected infant, found in a field still in her own blood. God said to Israel, "Live," and wiped off her blood. Israel grew into adolescence, forming breasts and long hair, now ready for ornaments and beauty. God spread his skirt over this foundling and made a covenant comparable to marriage. But as God adorned Israel with jewelry and cosmetics, she used these to prostitute herself. Her lovers did not give the way God did, but she kept on prostituting herself. So God will judge her as a wife caught in adultery. She will go into exile with sister Sodom. But God will remember his covenant with Israel before the end and he will restore (Ezek 16:1-63).

It is important to rehearse some of these stories from Israel's prophets because at times Yeshua's stories seem audacious or even cruel. Yet in a long line of holy men, Yeshua told the truth about his generation and saw through false piety. He told the story honestly and with unflattering details. Not least of Yeshua's prophetic stories is the one known as the Prodigal Son.

A Story Within a Story

N.T. Wright's reading of the Prodigal Son story (*Jesus and the Victory of God*, pp.125-131) makes good use of the drama of Israel's shame and restoration that was so on the minds of Yeshua's hearers. I will examine the story in much the same way as Wright, except in his over-emphasis on Yeshua's belief that the restoration happened at that time and his implication that Israel's hope has already been fulfilled.

Yeshua sat at table with sinners. He welcomed people who had grossly insulted his Father with rebellion, injustice, and even in cases bloodshed. He told parables about those forgiven much who in turn refused to forgive those who owed little. He condemned a generation which wanted restoration and an end to the shame of exile, but which readily condemned others to humiliation and the certain expectation of judgment. Yeshua's story of the Prodigal Son and the elder brother is ironic. Those who understood it must have been outraged.

A son, in effect, told his father he was impatient waiting for his inheritance. You may as well be dead to me, was the impetus of the son's demand for his share of the estate and his decision to leave his father. The son went out into far countries and fell into a low time.

What few had noticed before Wright put the Prodigal Son parable in the context of prophetic storytelling is that the prodigal's life is like Israel's. Israel was sent into far countries to be shamed. Israel had been radically ungrateful to the God who made her a people of promise. Moses' image of Israel's shameful exile involved being made jealous by a non-chosen people (Deut 32:21). The Assyrians, Babylonians, and others subjugated Israel in exile. In Yeshua's story, that shame is evoked with the atrocious image of a Jewish son feeding pigs for a gentile master.

Another thing largely unnoticed is that the father's implausible mercy did not wait for the son's return on the road. In the very act of giving the son the inheritance early, the father was inconceivably generous.

The return of the son to his family's home is a potential source of embarrassment for the father. Yet the father thinks nothing of it. He runs, which as Wright observes is very undignified for a head of a family. Instead of hiding the son away, the father throws a party for the whole town. The extreme mercy and generosity of God is also effectively portrayed in Yeshua's telling of the story. He himself had lived this mercy out by inviting sinners to his table and offering them a place in the kingdom.

The irony of the story comes as the older brother is angry, resentful, and jealous. He does not think the prodigal young man should be welcomed back. The elder is the one who stayed and who has kept working. Why should the younger get this treatment, being restored to dignity by the father and showered with gifts and adulation?

Again, what is unique in Wright's reading of the Prodigal Son parable is how Yeshua is taking Israel's story and giving it a vicious twist. Israel had been shamed into exile and at least part of the people had returned in the days of Zerubbabel, Ezra, and Nehemiah. What had the Israelite returnees found waiting for them: a people who had stayed and who did not welcome them back. Those who had stayed, the forbears of the Samaritans, resisted the return in both Ezra and Nehemiah's time. They did not welcome back their long lost brothers.

Clearly Yeshua is pointing to his own opponents as the elder brother in the story. And the prodigal brother is the band of sinners and disciples following Yeshua. This means Yeshua is calling the leaders of his generation Samaritans. They are now like the ones who stayed and did not welcome back the exiles. Yeshua has brought sinners out of exile into a place in the kingdom, but his opponents will not have it. They do not believe God should have mercy on these sinners. They judge Yeshua as an enemy of God for dispensing mercy and grace to the undeserving.

This is especially interesting because Yeshua's generation is eager for the kingdom to arrive. They believe themselves still in exile. The agricultural, social, political, and spiritual renewals promised in the Israelite prophets have not come to pass. Rome rules Israel cruelly. Israel is not vindicated in the sight of the nations. Israel is not restored from exile in the full sense.

Should those who hope for divine mercy and favor refuse to recognize mercy and favor shown to others?

The Open-Ended Tale and Hope

The story of the prodigal ends one scene too early, as Wright also correctly observes. The drama ends in unresolved conflict. This is perhaps why so many who have made sermons on the story omitted the part about the older brother. The joyful reunion with the all-forgiving father is a more satisfying ending. But the resentment of the older brother is Yeshua's challenge to his generation. The story ends open, unresolved, still full of hope.

Where Wright misses a point, however, is in his implication, both in his reading of the prodigal story and throughout *Jesus and the Victory of God* that Israel has missed its chance. Yeshua brought the kingdom and the gatekeepers were too busy with other things to notice. Wright says, for example, that Yeshua is "reconstituting Israel around himself" (131). Later he says Israel's national hopes, according to Yeshua, are set aside (by God?, 637) and that Yeshua himself is a replacement for the Torah (647). He seems to mean that the new community Yeshua is forming replaces the community of Israel which God had previously formed. It does not seem to occur to Wright that the whole thing could be a both-and, not an either-or.

Will Yeshua's telling of the prodigal story allow for this kind of finality in God's dealing with Israel? Will the father who ran down the road to meet his shameful son not also redeem the older brother in the end? And can we not surmise that Yeshua saw his death and resurrection as ushering in the penultimate, but not yet the ultimate? We would have to look at other parts of Yeshua's teaching to look for signs. Did he believe that more was yet to come after his resurrection and vindication? If so, then the point of Yeshua's ironic telling of this story is to waken his hearers, not to finally condemn.

Implications for Yeshua's Aims and Message

There are a number of things the prodigal story tells us about how Yeshua viewed his mission. First, it helps us realize that Yeshua saw his generation as being in exile, waiting for soon-coming deliverance. This reinforces the point, which can be seen again and again in the gospels, that Yeshua came as a liberator of his nation. The extension of the mission of the disciples to the nations, to the Gentiles, to the forbears of modern Christianity, spreads out from Yeshua's intention to save his own nation.

Second, from the vision of the father's boundless and unhesitating forgiveness, we can guess that this explains Yeshua's dining with sinners. It was a deliberate message of God's wide-ranging mercy and extraordinary favor. Yeshua demonstrated his belief by his practice.

Third, Yeshua saw his generation as hypocritically desiring God's favor while denying it to others. Similarly he told stories of those forgiven much who insisted on collecting everything owed them by others. He insisted that God forgives those who forgive others. And at his own death, he readily forgave his own tormentors. It is difficult to overstate the mercy and favor of God that Yeshua believed in.

Fourth, Yeshua warned his generation of missing a chance to collaborate with God, of enjoying the new age of kingdom blessings he was about to bring. In spite of God's far-reaching mercy, he does allow people to exclude themselves from blessing. The prodigal son was away for a long time, by his own choice. And it is likely that some prodigals never return. The father does not make them come home. So, whether temporarily or permanently, Yeshua saw many in his nation missing out on the fatted calf.

Fifth, Yeshua saw a coming change in leadership, that Israel's spiritual destiny was going to rest in the hands of the radically forgiven and not the old guard. Much of the debate about whether Yeshua intended to start a church or a new religion has missed an essential fact. The next generation of leaders, the ones Yeshua was handing off to, were all from Israel. They would send the movement out to the nations from Jerusalem. So the question of the emergence of the Church has become confused by the Jewish-Christian divide. Yeshua definitely intended to start a movement, a renewed people who would also dine with sinners and bring God's banquet to the world.

Yeshua as prophet used all the elements that were familiar: sonship, inheritance, exile to a far country, shame, return, welcome, and restoration. But he challenged those who put their hopes in restoration, vindication, and national glory not to resist when God did this very thing in unexpected ways. A people forgiven much must also forgive much in others. Otherwise, they would miss the celebration, the fatted calf, the rejoicing of life returned from death.

Chapter 10

Beatitudes of Hope
Matthew 5:1-12

The Beatitudes, as they are traditionally know, are Yeshua's most famous sayings. Everyone has heard such lines as, "Blessed are the meek, for they will inherit the earth." But what do these short sayings have to do with Yeshua's Jewish context? How would his audience have heard them? What is going on with the Sermon on the Mount?

Matthew's gospel, where we read the Beatitudes, is arranged thematically according to W.D. Davies and Dale Allison. They note that Matthew begins by establishing the back-story, the divinely sent identity of Yeshua in the stories of his birth, fleeing to Egypt, baptism, and temptation (63-4). Yeshua as the new Moses is set on the stage of a parallel narrative to Israel's story. The next step, for one who has been through Egypt, passed through the waters, been tried in the wilderness, is a teaching, and instruction, a Torah like Israel's on Sinai. The early outline of Matthew is identity and back story (chs. 1-4), teaching (chs. 5-7), signs and wonders (chs. 8-9), and signs and wonders by his disciples (ch. 10).

The Sermon on the Mount, then, represents a demonstration of the authority and message of Yeshua. It is part of a programmatic presentation of Yeshua in Matthew that follows a simple outline in the first ten chapters: identity, teaching, deeds, disciples.

Another scholar famous for his work on the Sermon on the Mount is Hans Dieter Betz. He suggests, as do others, that the Sermon on the Mount is not to be thought of as the exact address or outline Yeshua used on one occasion when speaking. A number of factors give evidence that the Sermon on the Mount is an ancient summary of the many things Yeshua taught, compiled by someone after Yeshua's time (*Essays on the Sermon on the Mount*). For one thing, there is the fact that the Sermon on the Mount is very similar to Luke's Sermon on the Plain. Yet comparison of the two stories shows that they are not the same event. And differences between the two show that Yeshua spoke about certain topics repeatedly.

In other words, you can make a pretty good case that the Sermon on the Mount is a sort of summation of the life message of Yeshua prepared after him by his disciples.

And the Beatitudes occupy a very important place in the Sermon on the Mount. They introduce the essential message of Yeshua. They are the epitome of what he stood for.

> Blessed are the poor in spirit, for theirs is the kingdom of heaven.
>
> Blessed are those who mourn, for they shall be comforted.
>
> Blessed are the meek, for they shall inherit the earth.
>
> Blessed are those who hunger and thirst for righteousness, for they shall be satisfied.
>
> Blessed are the merciful, for they shall obtain mercy.
>
> Blessed are the pure in heart, for they shall see God.
>
> Blessed are the peacemakers, for they shall be called sons of God.
>
> Blessed are those who are persecuted for righteousness' sake, for theirs is the kingdom of heaven.
>
> Blessed are you when men revile you and persecute you and utter all kinds of evil against you falsely on my account.
>
> Rejoice and be glad, for your reward is great in heaven, for so men persecuted the prophets who were before you.
>
> –Matthew 5:3-12, RSV

The Beatitudes represent several things:

1. The *essence* of Yeshua's way for his disciples.

2. The *promise* of the coming kingdom.

3. Command or *wisdom* for living in light of the reality of the coming kingdom.

4. The *reality* of the present age.

5. *Antithesis* to common ways of thinking about life, religion, and piety.

I will consider each of these five in light of the context of Yeshua's time and also the time of the generation after him, when Matthew was written and began to circulate. Saving the best for last, I will explore the promise, wisdom, reality, and antithesis aspects before coming back to the essence of Yeshua's way.

The Promise of the Coming Kingdom

The kingdom promise of the Beatitudes cannot be overemphasized. Yeshua's teaching began with a message that the kingdom of heaven was at hand, about to appear. As we have seen many times in examining Yeshua's context, his deeds and words are all about the promises of God for renewal and the completion and healing of the world coming to pass. Yeshua taught and modeled a life based on the better world God is preparing.

In the beatitudes, we get a number of images of the world to come:

• *theirs is the kingdom of heaven:* Yeshua declares a verdict. The poor in spirit will receive or enter the kingdom of heaven. The seriousness with which we take this promise depends on our evaluation of Yeshua's authority. For Matthew and his community, it was a given that Yeshua's authority was divine, unquestionable. If Yeshua said the poor in spirit will receive and enter the kingdom, then it is so. But, as we will see, this is an antithesis, a contrary way of looking at life and religion.

• *they shall be comforted:* The future tense of this saying implies that it will happen in the world to come. It follows the logic of the first Beatitude. The coming kingdom will be comfort. People mourn because of death and suffering. Yeshua's promise is that these will have no place in the world to come. The implication is that this future blessing affects quality of life in the present, not only in the future.

• *they shall inherit the earth*: This may seem confusing to readers whose idea of afterlife is otherworldly and non-material. For Yeshua's Jewish hearers, there was no difficulty here. The earth is the place that will be renewed. The coming kingdom is on earth. The phrase "kingdom of heaven" may further the confusion for modern readers. But in Jewish context, "heaven" was understood as a indirect term for God. "Kingdom of heaven" should not communicate an otherworldly place in the clouds, but the reign of God as king on earth. Therefore, when Yeshua says the meek, a synonym for poor in spirit, will inherit the earth, he means the same as in the first beatitude: they will receive and enter the kingdom.

• *they shall be satisfied*: Again, the future tense implies this will happen in the age to come. The frustration of thwarted righteousness in this age, the darkening of every good motive, the constantly foiled desire for pure goodness, will not exist in the coming world. Purity and unspoiled virtue will be the norm.

• *they shall obtain mercy*: In the coming world, those who gave mercy here will receive mercy from God. It will be seen in our further investigation below, this is not simply a mathematical formula. It is not as if the righteous will receive only the mercy they earned on earth by showing it to others. The saying has a general wisdom meaning, describing the character of those who will receive and enter the kingdom.

• *they shall see God*: In the coming age, these will see God in some literal sense. This represents a heightening of the promise. We have moved from receiving and entering the kingdom, to being comforted, satisfied, shown mercy, and now even to seeing God. The progression in the promises of the Beatitudes is good literary or rhetorical form, increasing the delight of the reader or hearer throughout the discourse.

• *they shall be called sons of God*: "Sons of" is an ancient idiom for "belonging to the set of." That is, these shall belong to the family or species of God. This is deification. The idea is likely that those who engage in divine-like activity in this age, bringing healing and peace to relationships, are the same ones who will be transformed into divine character in the coming age. The promise is to be like God, to be intimately related to him.

• *theirs is the kingdom of heaven:* Though this repeats the first Beatitude's promise, the context has now changed subtly. What is true of the poor in spirit is also true of those persecuted for righteousness. If the humble and lowly receive and enter the kingdom, that is exaltation. If those persecuted receive and enter the kingdom, that is reversal. It is too easy to believe the judgments of others, but if we accept the authority of Yeshua, we believe that God's judgment in the coming age is based on better criteria than the judgment we face from people in this age.

• *your reward is great in heaven:* Again, in Jewish modes of expression from Yeshua's time, heaven more likely represents the heavenly tribunal and not the place of afterlife. Thus, this saying most specifically means "your reward is great in the judgment of God" and not "in the afterlife." The promise is especially potent since we do not know what divine rewards will be like, but we can imagine they will exceed all of our hopes and dreams.

Command or Wisdom for Living in Light of the Reality of the Coming Kingdom

In addition to the promise aspect of the Beatitudes, Yeshua's sayings also concern ethical and wise living:

• *the poor in spirit:* Some see this as deliberately targeting the spoken or unspoken assumption that those blessed are the rich. It is possible that "poor in spirit" is a precisely worded phrase intended to circumvent the naive idea that mere poverty is a blessing. In wisdom sayings, such clarity is not always needed. Thus, in Luke's version we read "blessed are the poor." Both sayings are antitheses or reversals of normal expectation. The lowly and humble tend to have greater blessings because God exalts those who humble themselves. Self-exaltation is a futile effort. The wisdom of Yeshua is to let other people and God bless us rather than seeking to bless ourselves.

• ***those who mourn:*** There is no virtue in mourning or being a mourner. Even people given to evil and cruelty mourn when they suffer loss. The wisdom here is twofold. First, when the righteous mourn, it is mourning with hope. Death and suffering are not the last word. Second, those who live in light of the values of the kingdom will comfort mourners. Yeshua taught his disciples to work toward making the blessings of the kingdom present in this age.

• ***the meek:*** This is virtually identical to the expression "poor in spirit." While poor in spirit emphasizes poverty and humility, meekness emphasizes powerlessness. The problems of poverty, lowliness, and powerlessness are related. But the wisdom is in knowing that the power that matters is not our own.

• ***those who hunger and thirst for righteousness:*** The idea is that righteousness is not found in this age, or at least not pure righteousness. Our own motives and those of others are always suspect. The wisdom of this saying is that the good we imagine must really exist somewhere. The fact that we can imagine it should suggest that such purity and goodness is real. The longing is not false and it will be satisfied. So in the present age, longing and seeking after it is righteousness, even though our desire is mixed with impure motives. If we accept Yeshua's authority, this is a divine stamp of approval on our present efforts, imperfect as they are.

• ***the merciful:*** Yeshua's teaching in many places is that God forgives the forgiving. This raises questions. Is God's forgiveness for every sin except unforgiveness? Is mercilessness unforgivable? If so, is anyone in the clear? Knowing the radical mercy of God, expressed in Yeshua's words and deeds, such as dining with sinners, it seems best to take this in a general sense and not as an absolute and unforgiving rule. At the very least, however, Yeshua's teaching should make us wonder what judgment we will face for our lack of mercy toward others. Mercy is the way of Yeshua and all who follow him.

• *the pure in heart:* Yeshua spoke elsewhere of having a singular focus, that is, being directed toward God and his will on earth. The pure in heart are likely those who place the kingdom first, before all other concerns. The undivided heart has no place for idols, including greed and pride. This is a high and difficult calling. Some have seen the Beatitudes as increasing in difficulty from beginning to end.

• *peacemakers:* Yeshua elsewhere speaks of making right any offenses we have caused others, of confronting those who have done wrong, and of forgiving and reconciling relationships. God is healing the rift between good and evil and Yeshua's followers are called to heal and not further conflict and evil. It is not necessary to interpret this absolutely. Yeshua called for conflict in certain cases (persecution for righteousness, opposing cruelty, etc.). Peacemaking is the higher aim even when conflict is called for.

• *persecuted for righteousness' sake:* The key phrase is "for righteousness' sake." When persecution is the result of agendas opposed to faith and goodness, the persecuted can take comfort in knowing they are not receiving divine judgment. A life lived for God will not necessarily be appreciated by all or rewarded by society. Goodness makes evil envious.

• *when men revile you . . . utter evil against you:* The righteous may be troubled by condemnation from other people and earthly authorities. Yeshua's disciples should know that it is only God's judgment that matters. In every case of conflict, wisdom is to consider what God's judgment will be. Slander and abuse from people hurts, but will not last and will not carry the day when all is said and done.

The Reality of the Present Age

There are those who believe Yeshua was a mistaken prophet. He came, some would say, to announce that the kingdom was arriving through his work and all the promises of God were being fulfilled. He died and nothing changed. His resurrection, some would say, is a paltry substitute for the better world he spoke of.

Where is the kingdom? How is the longing for righteousness being satisfied? Where is the comfort, the end of all mourning, the reward from God?

Yeshua's teaching is read too simplistically by many of his interpreters. He spoke often of the reality of the present age and of the delay of the kingdom. The strong promise of the nearness of the kingdom stands in tension with many examples of the harshness of the present age. In the Hebrew Bible this kind of tension in prophetic promises juxtaposed with denunciations of present corruption was common.

It is not necessary to see Yeshua as a failed idealist. The Beatitudes are among the sayings of Yeshua that speak of delay, of the ideal put off and evil continuing. There will be the poor, mourners, those whose longings for true goodness are frustrated with sheer vanity and the poisoning of all things. Persecution is going to happen after Yeshua leaves. The ideal will not come right away.

Antithesis to Common ways of Thinking about Life, Religion, and Piety

It is a common poison in religion for the values of power, greed, and pride to take hold even in holy places. Yeshua would not be alone by any means in criticizing the leaders of his generation. Corruption, infighting, and personal competitions for power were talked about before Yeshua's time, in Yeshua's time, and it as the verdict of the rabbinic community after Yeshua that the downfall of the Temple was due to these things.

That the Beatitudes are reversals, antitheses, should not go unnoticed. The thinking, spoken or unspoken, of most people is that the signs of greatness are wealth, confidence, ambition, the will to rise to the top, compromise, and devotion to the principle of success. Leaders, it is thought, must face reality and do what is necessary for the greater good. Those who have small followings, whose words are not widely listened to, are not great leaders. Their lack of success reveals their failure.

Yeshua's wisdom is not opposed to success or acclaim. Thousands came out to hear him speak and to witness his signs and wonders. So neither should we assume that popularity is a sign of evil.

The signs are not success or acclaim, but a character defined by Hebrew wisdom. Yeshua's words are an interpretation of the tradition of Proverbs, Ecclesiastes, and Job. It is better to be a sufferer than one who makes others suffer. It is better to be lowly than prideful. It is better to allow love to heal relationships than to promote strife. It is better to know the good and pursue it with all our resources, as if it were treasure for which we would sell all to obtain it. Greed and ambition are false masters, since nothing satisfies. The poor are not destitute because they deserve it necessarily. Time and chance happen to us all. Better a modest lifestyle and goodness than riches poisoned with malice and vanity.

While Temple authorities compromised with Romans and pursued power and greed in Yeshua's time, the lowly Israelite, trusting in God's promises, was far better off. To hear from a divinely sent authority that poverty, mourning, powerlessness, and even persecution were not God's final word was a comfort.

Yeshua's words endure as a challenge to leaders in every aspect of life. They also endure as a challenge to every person—mother, father, son, daughter—to find wiser purposes in life.

The Essence of Yeshua's Way for His Disciples

Yeshua located his messianic mission especially in Isaiah 61. In Luke, this shows up in a story about Yeshua reading the scroll of prophets in the synagogue (Luke 4:16-30). In Matthew it shows up in some of the language of the Beatitudes and also in 11:5, where Yeshua answers a query by John the Baptist: "the poor have good news preached to them."

Isaiah 61 language comes up in the Beatitudes as well. Yeshua tells the poor, or poor in spirit, that they will receive and enter the kingdom. Yeshua comforts mourners with future promise. Yeshua tells good news to those persecuted, afflicted, left behind by a society bent on ambition and power.

The most important thing to note about the Beatitudes is that they relate this life to the life to come. The promises of the coming kingdom of God affect how we view wisdom and ethics in this life as well as how we view suffering in this present age.

To put it simply, Yeshua's way for his disciples is: live as much as possible as though the kingdom is near or has already arrived.

He brings together in one short set of saying the blessings of Israelite prophecy and the ethical astuteness of Israelite wisdom literature. But, if Israel already had the prophets and the sages of the wisdom literature, why the need for Yeshua's Beatitudes?

Yeshua adds two things. First, he presents us with the crux of all the Hebrew scriptures in shorter and more memorable form. Second, he gives the authority of a divinely sent agent to these teachings of comfort and farsightedness. Matthew has built into his presentation of the Beatitudes a clear statement that the one saying these things is one sent by God, the beloved son, the new Moses and the new David.

And the Beatitudes are far more than just one of Yeshua's teachings. They are the introduction to the Sermon on the Mount. The Sermon on the Mount is an ancient, perhaps more ancient than Matthew says Hans Dieter Betz, collection of teachings that show the essence of Yeshua's message (*Essays on the Sermon on the Mount*). The Sermon on the Mount is the essence and the Beatitudes are the quintessence.

They help us locate the aim and teaching of Yeshua in his context. They show us that he stands in the Israelite tradition and speaks with authority as one qualified to give the ultimate expression to that tradition. The Beatitudes are not the word of a simple teacher. They are words from God and are recognized as such by those who agree with Matthew about the identity of Yeshua.

Chapter 11

Seeds and Fruit
Mark 4:1-20

Some people assume that Yeshua was a simple teacher, that his words were for peasants' ears, used homey object lessons, and could be comprehended easily. It might seem unfair if the healing and compassionate prophet-messiah had an inside group or if he used language that would be hard for crowds to grasp, requiring private explanations to the inner circle.

Yet that is exactly what Yeshua did. He said to his inner circle, "The secret of the kingdom of God has been given to you, but to those outside, everything is in parables" (Mark 4:11).

No doubt there are many reasons for the dual audience scenario. For one thing, Yeshua was building a movement and said so on many occasions. A movement requires teaching and direction. Crowds who come out for a day will not be able to hear an in-depth explanation of the goals and methods of the movement. For another, Yeshua's message was one that could easily be misunderstood. In fact, Yeshua's own inner circle continued to misunderstand him until after the resurrection. Certain prevalent ideas about Messiah and the kingdom of God predisposed Yeshua's hearers to expect something that would not, in fact, happen.

So, the crowds who attended Yeshua's outdoor speeches heard many intriguing, inviting similes and stories, but would have needed more time and explanation to penetrate their meaning. They heard mysterious sayings about vineyards and kings and servants. Only after many stories and repetitions would it become clear who these kings and servants were and why Yeshua used the old prophetic metaphor of a vineyard.

The inner circle got private explanations. They heard teachings repeated with variations. No doubt the figures of speech became clearer with time. Yeshua's use and reuse of tropes from the Israelite prophets and the wisdom literature of Israel were not simple. They could be interpreted in many different ways (and have been in the history of interpretation ever since).

To understand Yeshua, his original hearers had the context of Israel's story and Israel's scriptures as their foundation. Some of the ensuing confusion in interpreting Yeshua ever since then has come from assumptions that Yeshua was speaking about matters important to the developing church of Christendom instead of groups of Israelites in the first century.

Yeshua's hearers also had another clue to the meaning of all his stories and similes. The central theme was the coming reign of God on earth (the kingdom). Yet even here Yeshua was confusing, because this kingdom talk did not go in expected directions. Almost always there was a twist, a turning, an unexpected conclusion. Yeshua often spoke of delay in the kingdom, of the expected subjects of the kingdom being excluded, of the expected delinquents of the kingdom being the true subjects, of the greater receptivity of the lowly, of the obstinate blindness of the privileged, and of a suffering king instead of a triumphant one.

"Do you not understand?" Yeshua often asked his confused inner circle. "Let he one who has ears to hear listen," he urged. "Take my yoke and learn from me," he invited, "you will find rest for your souls." He promised solid assurance, an eternal dwelling built on a rock for those who heard and practiced his words. But it took much listening and concentration to understand. And they did not, until after the great event that changed everything, the resurrection of the Son of God.

But Yeshua's dual-audience approach recruited passionate followers. They heard insider language. "I am the vine and you are the branches," Yeshua summoned to his disciples. Happy are servants doing their master's will when he returns. Yours is to inherit the earth. You will see God. You have found a treasure in a field and it is worth selling all to have it. To you it has been given to know the secrets of the kingdom of God.

Clues to the Sower Parable

Standing beside the lake of Galilee, Yeshua spun a homey yarn about a farmer sowing seed. Galilee was and still is an agricultural area. The crowds and the inner circle hearing Yeshua no doubt saw furrowed rows, green crops, and verdant orchards as Yeshua spoke. To the crowd there were many puzzles in Yeshua's story. A sower, seed? Who and what is he talking about?

The crowds came to see him heal. They came to see if he was a prophet like John or a king to lead against Rome. The air was pregnant with expectation. Seeds were being planted. Some bore fruit but most were eaten by birds, stunted by the ever-present rocks of Galilean soil, or choked by weeds. This had to have something to do with a clash of power, the kingdom, faith in God, success or failure in the crop.

Apocalyptic images with stages or multiple parts were known. N.T. Wright uses the example of Daniel and the four-part statue from the second chapter of the book of Daniel (*Jesus and the Victory of God*, 231). Daniel's teaching, like Yeshua's, was about "mysteries" (Dan 2:28) and the kingship of God. Daniel's teaching was about a "kingdom that will never be destroyed" (Dan 2:44). Like the Sower Parable, the vision in Daniel 2 had four parts. Each part led progressively toward the finale, which was the coming of the kingdom.

As Wright says, there is much in Daniel 2 that is different from Mark 4. Daniel's vision is about successive kingdoms whereas Mark 4 is about four conditions existing simultaneously. A statue is a very different image from an agricultural field. Yet the idea of mysterious stories with four parts as lessons of the kingdom was nothing new. And apocalyptic tales were still being written, and perhaps told by word of mouth, in Judea and in Galilee, where revolution was festering and would come in one generation. Surely Yeshua's story had something to do with revolution, Israel's story, God's expectation of the people.

The context of the parable also likely brought to mind the idea of seed, an image with associations in the story of Israel. The seed of Abraham was a description of Israel (Wright, 232). Psalm 126, a Psalm of Ascents, spoke of one who went out weeping with a bag of seed but came home rejoicing with sheaves of grain in hand. Israel in exile wept, but the seed was planted, and would bear a crop, and that crop would be restoration of the nation and great joy in Zion. Ezra complained of the seed of Israelite descent being mixed with foreign seed (Ezra 9:2). And most importantly, for N.T. Wright's interpretation of the Sower Parable, is Isaiah 6:13.

Isaiah 6 was an important chapter, the one in which Isaiah saw God's robe in the Temple and had his lips burned with coal by a seraph. Yeshua alluded already to one part of Isaiah 6 in revealing the meaning of the Sower Parable to his inner circle (compare Mark 14:12 and Isa 6:9-10). It may very well be, as is often the case in Jewish midrashic thinking (see chapter 15 for more about midrash and the gospels), that Yeshua had other parts of Isaiah 6 in mind too. We read there that the prophet was called to speak truth to a people that would not listen, instructed about the coming exile of Israel, and promised that a "holy seed" would remain in the cut off stump of Israel. As Wright says, "Within second-Temple Judaism, the idea of 'seed' is capable of functioning as a shorthand for the 'remnant' who will return when the exile is finally over" (232).

Some might object that the Sower Parable says the seed is the word, not the remnant of Israel that remains faithful to God. Many think of "the word" as a reference to the scriptures. Wright anticipates this objection and notes another important Isaiah message, from chapter 55, in which the "word will not return void." The word in Isaiah 55 is the word of Israel's return, in joy, to the land and to blessing (Wright, 233). The seed and the word in the Sower Parable are the word of good news, that exile is over, that Israel is restored to blessing (a specific word, then, and not a term for the whole of the scriptures). That is the word the crowds in

Galilee hope to hear about. That is the word the inner circle of Yeshua wants to hear as well.

But the Sower Parable will not go in the direction that either the crowds or the inner circle want. It will twist and turn and become confusing. The complexity of the subverted story of Israel's return from exile is perhaps what has caused interpreters of the Sower Parable ever since Yeshua to miss its meaning. Yeshua is not a simple teacher. Let those with ears to hear listen closely.

Twists in the Sower Parable

In the common thinking of the people, the kingdom of God would come suddenly and completely. One day the people would be oppressed and burdened with foreign rule and then the kingdom of Israel would rise meteorically and smash the foreheads of Moab and Seth (see Num 24:17). In the second Jewish revolt, around the year 130 C.E., people even gave the name "Son of the Star" (Bar Kochva) to the rebel leader, Simon. Expectation was of either a human or heavenly king leading the people to victory and a new age. The change would be drastic, complete.

If Yeshua's Sower Parable is about the end of the exile and the word of Israel's restoration, it disappoints expectant crowds with frustrating incompleteness, delay, and upheaval. The word of restoration, the seed, does not bring a complete crop. Birds eat it, rocks prevent its growth, and weeds choke it out. Only some of the seed grows to bear fruit.

To put it in the simplest terms, Yeshua spoke of a penultimate stage, a coming of the kingdom in part, an age to come being realized progressively instead of suddenly. This does not indicate that Yeshua had given up on the sudden and dramatic reversal of evil at the end of the age. In other places he spoke of the sharp and decisive victory of the Son of Man. A day would come when the sheep would be separated from the goats. The Son of Man would be seen coming on the clouds. The coming of the Son of Man would be like lightning, visible to all. The elect would be gathered from the four winds. Those who endure to the end will be saved. About that day and hour no one knows, but the Father.

So it is not that the Sower Parable denies the story Israel is waiting for. It is, rather, that the Sower Parable, introduces a new part of the story, a time of partial realization. The kingdom of God is near, not far. It is at hand, but not for all. It is coming now, for those who let the seed fall on willing hearts.

Yeshua is bringing the kingdom as his hearers listen. He is headed to a final confrontation that will inaugurate a new age beginning with his own resurrection.

But many people will never even receive the word of restoration, of all things made new. The birds, which Yeshua told his inner circle represent the evil powers allied with Satan, will steal the word before it can germinate. Many things keep Israelites (and other people in the long history since Yeshua) from even considering the restoration of Israel and the nations in the person of Yeshua.

Others would receive the idea in a shallow way, but lay it aside with no struggle to persevere. The crowds who hear Yeshua's similes and stories will be excited about revolution and change, but will not follow through. There is much interest, but not much tenacity of faith. Will the Son of Man find faith on the earth when he returns?

Still others would embrace the word of restoration and follow it, but allow fear, affluence, misplaced priorities, and other concerns to smother their dedication. They will not bear fruit either, even though they have believed the message of restoration in Yeshua. They did not believe it enough to sell everything and hold on to the treasure.

But the return from exile, the restoration of blessing, will happen for those who receive Yeshua's teaching, practice it, and bear fruit. Far from the sudden, dramatic reversal the hearers of Yeshua desire, the kingdom he is preaching is penultimate, partial, preparatory. While we wait during the long delay of the ultimate kingdom, a foreshadowing of its blessing exists in the community of those who bear fruit the way Yeshua taught.

In that community, mourners are comforted. Hunger for righteousness is filled. The meek are busy inheriting the earth, not by avaricious grasping, but by faithful serving.

That They May Not Perceive

In Isaiah 6, as the prophet is commissioned, he is told to speak the truth but to ironically tell the people not to listen. The message in Isaiah's time is that judgment, not restoration, is inevitable for his generation. It is not that God does not want people to hear and be healed from evil and suffering. In fact, some did listen to Isaiah and a community of the faithful did exist in Isaiah's Israel. By telling Isaiah to say, "hear and hear, but do not understand" (6:9, RSV), God is foretelling the inevitability of judgment for that generation. Isaiah will speak truth that will largely be rejected. But, though exile and shame are inevitable, the stump of Judah has a holy seed ready to grow after the exile. Judgment is not the last word.

In Yeshua's generation, his message would also be largely rejected. But his message was dangerous, as was Isaiah's in his time. Rulers like Herod Antipas and Pontius Pilate and Caiphas the High Priest would hear revolutionary talk. Wright says, "if too many understand too well, the prophet's liberty of movement, and perhaps life, may be cut short" (237).

So Yeshua's talks were coded language. They could not be pinned down as talk of war. The crowds were drawn to hear such talk and also to revive hope in divine miracles and blessings, but the twists, turns, and riddles would cause all but the inner circle to misunderstand, to be stupefied by mysteries.

From Crowd to Insider

But the Sower Parable illustrates Yeshua's method of drawing those from the crowds to the inner circle. After talks with the crowd, Yeshua would withdraw with his inner circle. He did not invite only the twelve. Mark 4:10 says that the twelve and those who gathered around Yeshua heard the private explanation. To these, the twelve and the others who came for the private explanation, was given "the secrets of the kingdom."

The invitation at the end of the coded parable was there: "He who has ears to hear, let him hear" (Mark 4:9, RSV). To those who responded to this summons, birds were explained as Satan, rocks were shallow faith, and weeds were revealed as affluence and detours away from singular purpose in life.

Through repetition and invitations to the inner circles, Yeshua taught a clearer message to some. He gave them words that he promised would be like a rock on which to build a house. He taught an easy yoke that would set them free. He gave the secrets of the kingdom away.

Without denying the ultimate kingdom, the age to come when all exile will be ended and when the goodness intended from the beginning by God is at last realized, Yeshua invited the crowds to join a different kind of revolution. Wherever Yeshua went, the kingdom was present. Those who were blind regained sight. Those who were poor were blessed. Those who were in mourning found comfort and even life from the dead.

The Sower Parable is a message that the ultimate kingdom will be delayed. The sons of the kingdom should look to bear fruit and in that fruit will be the end of exile and the beginning of restoration. Much of Yeshua's teaching dealt with the formation of a community. Yeshua's mother and daughters and sisters and brothers are those who do the will of God. Yeshua's congregation has rules about forgiveness and mercy and reconciliation.

The scandal in Yeshua's story, the one that causes most to let the seed be snatched by birds, is that the world goes on with its evil and suffering intact. The life, death, and resurrection of Yeshua brought no visible change. The seed of restoration seems to have fallen off the path.

But the hard message of the Sower Parable is that restoration is actually here for those who receive Yeshua's words and use them to bear fruit. Kingdom blessings do not wait completely for the age to come. They can be realized in part now in the community that Yeshua called to be the remnant of Israel and to spread to all nations.

Chapter 12

Wicked Tenants
Mark 12:1-12

A recurring and definitive question in reading the story of Yeshua is where he placed himself in relation to the Israelite people and Judaism, on the one hand, and the new community he envisioned coming after him, on the other. When reading controversy stories, should we assume that later Christians are speaking through Yeshua, putting, as it were, words in his mouth? Or is it realistic to read Yeshua as forming a renewal movement within Judaism (and also one that will go beyond it)? Is he forming something other than Judaism to replace it or something within Judaism to renew it?

A long tradition of academic interpreters finds in stories critical of Israelite leaders, denouncing priests and Pharisees and enacting protests at the Temple, the voice of Christians, writing the gospels after the Temple is destroyed and reflecting division and feuding between Judaism and its new stepsister. But theories based on speculations about dates are far less conclusive than they sound, whereas reading stories for internal and external coherence often brings more promising results. In other words, if the stories of Yeshua's controversy with his own generation makes sense in the bigger story of Second Temple Judaism, then there is no reason to assign his words and ideas to later Christians.

This question about Yeshua's relationship to the Jewish people of his time, and his view of the Jewish people's relationship with God, is definitive in several ways. First, it affects our idea of the accuracy of the stories we have about Yeshua. Are they realistic or anachronistic? Second, the modern world, with intervening centuries of separation, tragedy, and enmity between Christians and Jews has colored our thinking as readers. How can we find Yeshua in his context when we're conditioned to think of Yeshua as opposed to Judaism or supplanting it?

One of the clearest and harshest stories Yeshua told in condemning his generation was that of the Wicked Tenants (Mark 12:1-12 and also Matt 21:33-40 and Luke 20:9-16). It is a story which has much potential to be read as some sort of Christian invective or triumphal tale of replacement. It is also very much a story about the identity of Yeshua, his exalted authority and role. It is all too easy to combine the two, to think that any high view of Yeshua's identity is post-Jewish and belongs together with the story of Christianity replacing Judaism as the chosen faith. And, conversely, any story faithful to Yeshua's Jewish context, it might be assumed, would then opt for a low view of his identity—a mistaken prophet unjustly condemned.

Internal Criticism in Israel, Calling Down Divine Judgment

Our understanding of Judaism in Yeshua's time is complicated by many things. There are a fair number of sources, but many of the sources are problematic in various ways. Some we do not know the time and author of and others we do know, but we have reason to doubt that their telling is without some deliberate distortions. The literature about Second Temple Judaism is massive.

Without attempting to understand the entire culture, religion, history, and sociology of Judaism in Yeshua's time, we can nonetheless learn from the many stories and writings that survive. A question helpful in locating Yeshua in this world and time is whether others, like him, criticized Israel harshly from within. And a simple reading of some of the literature from the time shows us that internal criticism, even damning disparagement, was not unheard of or, really, uncommon (Elliott, *The Survivors of Israel*).

One of the most judgmental sects in Yeshua's time wrote the literature referred to now as the Dead Sea Scrolls. This community spoke of the time of God's visitation in judgment. There would be war between the sons of light (the Community of the scrolls) and the sons of darkness. But unlike much other Jewish writing, the enemies of the righteous were not only or even primarily from outside of Israel. The most dangerous enemy, as far as they were concerned, was within.

In the *Manual of Discipline*, a document describing the requirements of the Community, the candidate was told to swear he would segregate himself from "the men of sin who walk along paths of irreverence" (1QS 5.10). These people, apparently unfaithful Israelites, were earning for themselves "everlasting annihilation." In the *Damascus Document*, also about community rules and values, this judgment is said to come upon "those entering the covenant but who did not remain steadfast" (CD 8.2).

In the various apocalyptic writings of the period, by authors unknown, we find many stories of divine judgment called down on the wicked within Israel. In one such story, the details are a bit like Yeshua's Wicked Tenants parable:

> Again I saw those sheep, how they went astray, going in
> diverse ways and abandoning that house of his. Then the
> Lord of the sheep called some from among the sheep and
> sent them to the sheep, but the sheep began to slay them
> . . .. He sent many other sheep to those sheep to testify to
> them and to lament over them. Thereafter I saw that when
> they abandoned the house of the Lord and his tower, they
> went astray completely, and their eyes became blindfolded.
> Then I saw the Lord of the sheep, how he executed much
> slaughter upon them . . . Then they burned that tower
> and plowed that house (1 Enoch 89:51-52, 54, 67, in
> Charlesworth, *The Old Testament Pseudepigrapha*, Vol. 1).

Earlier in 1 Enoch we read of Israelites who are not elect, who invite "eternal execration" on themselves and who will not find any mercy for themselves (5:4-7). Jubilees speaks of an "evil generation which sins in the land" and experiences pillaging and destruction (23:14-22).

In a text speaking about a messianic figure, the Son of David, we read that "there is no one among them [residents of Jerusalem] who practiced righteousness or justice: from their leader to the commonest of the people, they were in every kind of sin" (Psa of Sol 17:19-20, Charlesworth). This Son of David will not allow the wicked among Israel to dwell in his kingdom (17:26-27).

The protagonist Ezra in the book known as Fourth Ezra sees visions of Israel's judgment and laments that few will enjoy the world to come and most will be tormented in it (7:47-48). He sees "the failings of us who live in the land" and fears "the swiftness of the judgment that is to come" (8:15-18). In a similar book, another figure, Baruch, says simply, "those who sin, you blot out among your own" (2 Baruch 54:22, Charlesworth).

It is evident, then, that criticism of Israel, from within, was a well-known phenomenon. This will help us locate the Wicked Tenants parable as a kind of Jewish self-critical tale.

Tenants, Authority, Vineyard

Mark places Yeshua's telling of the Wicked Tenants in the context of controversies at the Temple, his cleansing of the Temple and the challenging of his authority by Temple leaders (as does Matthew and Luke). The Wicked Tenants is a controversy story even before it begins.

The story itself is simple: a vineyard owner leases the land to tenants and goes away. He sends a servant to get the required payment from the fruit. The servant is beaten. A second one is sent and gets hurt even worse. A third is killed. Many others are treated in the same way. So the vineyard owner sends his son, thinking this will up the stakes. But they kill the son too. And so what will the vineyard owner do, Yeshua asks? Will he not come and kill the tenants and give the vineyard to new owners? Isn't this just like Psalm 118:22-23? The leaders had no trouble understanding Yeshua was condemning them.

But the story raises some troubling questions. Not least is this one: what kind of vineyard owner sends his son when all these servants have been beaten and killed? And if the vineyard owner is God, the servants are the prophets, and the son is Yeshua, then aren't we wondering if God is a bad father? Who would do this to his son?

And there are others. Why does Yeshua choose a vineyard as his illustration? And why are the villains tenants, leasers of land? What is Yeshua saying about his relationship to God and to the prophets in this story? How does this story of the vineyard and the son lead to a saying about a stone?

The Vineyard

"Let me sing for my beloved a love song concerning his vineyard," says Isaiah (5:1, RSV). This is one of the easier occasions to be certain Yeshua is alluding to a text from the Hebrew Bible. The comparisons between Yeshua's story and Isaiah's are tight. Yeshua's story begins, "A man planted a vineyard, and set a hedge around it, and dug a pit for the wine press, and built a tower" (Mark 12:1, RSV). Isaiah's begins similarly, "He digged it and cleared it of stones, and planted it with choice vines; he built a watchtower in the midst of it" (5:2, RSV).

Isaiah's story is similar to Yeshua's. A vineyard owner prepared a choice vineyard and planted only the best grapes. Yet the vineyard angered and disappointed him, producing only worthless grapes. The speaker in Isaiah's story then becomes God addressing Israel directly. What will I do with you? What haven't I done for you? I will break down the wall and trample your ground. I will let thorns grow in it. The speaker again changes back to the prophet. God looked in his vineyard for justice but found only blood.

The plot lines of Isaiah's story and Yeshua's are similar: a vineyard is planted with optimism, the fruit expected is not delivered, so the end will be judgment—in Isaiah's story for the vineyard itself and in Yeshua's for the tenants. The difference is important. Isaiah's story foreshadowed the conquests of Assyria and Babylon which left Israel devastated. Yeshua's story foreshadowed the Roman destruction of the Temple and the city. Yet Yeshua's story is about judgment only of the tenant-farmers in charge and not of the vineyard itself. The leaders of Israel will be removed, but for the good of the vineyard, Israel, and not to harm the vineyard itself.

The Vineyard Owner

Scot McKnight comments on the "rather incomprehensible" vineyard owner "sending his son into the fray" thinking "somehow he will be treated more kindly" (*Jesus and His Death*, 152). He says: "The parable fits with other shocking statements by Jesus about how God deals with humans (cf. Luke 15:1-32)."

Yeshua's stories often cut more than one way and betray layers to those who look at them again and again. The Wicked Tenants is not merely a story of judgment. It is also a story reflecting either sarcastic irony or hidden motivations. What are Yeshua's hearers to think of this father who sends his son to a certain death? The sarcastic reading is that Yeshua is complaining, bucking against the impossible mission the vineyard owner has sent him on. Yet Yeshua elsewhere is resigned to his destiny and so it more consistent to read Yeshua's intention as irony, a desire to surprise the hearer, but not to protest his dire straits.

So can the vineyard owner's decision be explained? It can't. The story has an unresolved note about it, the mysterious action of a father which, in human terms, is unjustifiable. The son comes for the vineyard but only dies. As McKnight notes, in this story, Yeshua's death is not given any meaning (p. 152). It is not a saving death. The vineyard could have been saved without the son dying.

This parable is not about saving, but condemning. The death of the son does not condemn the vineyard, but it condemns the tenants. Yeshua has just come and threatened the most powerful icon of the Israelite leaders, the Temple economy. They have challenged his authority in turn and he knows they plan to kill him.

Beware, says Yeshua, for you are killing the vineyard owner's son. He is bound to be angry. He will destroy you. And it happened as Yeshua said only forty years later when the Romans came.

Prophets, the Son, and Yeshua

The Torah and prophets were until John, Yeshua said in Luke 16:16. Throughout the story of Yeshua, his role is very much that of a prophet. Whether he is like Elijah and Elisha—healing and doing nature miracles for the community of the faithful—or the classical prophets teaching and speaking for God, Yeshua's actions quite often fit into the role of a prophet.

Prophets called disciples, as Samuel, Elijah, and Elisha were known to do in the Hebrew Bible. Prophets denounced the comfortable and spoke up for the weak. Prophets foretold things like the coming war with Rome and the Temple destruction, just as Yeshua did. Prophets spoke God's words as his mouthpieces, as Yeshua was known to say what the Father showed him. Prophets, often enough, wound up dead.

"I shall send them witnesses . . . but they will not hear; and they will; even kill the witnesses" (Jubilees 1:12, Charlesworth). Josephus tells the history of wicked king Manasseh, who he says at one point killed a prophet each day and filled Jerusalem with blood (*Antiquities* 10:38). And there is the quintessential story of a prophet's murder, of Zechariah's murder, in 2 Chronicles 24:18-22.

Yeshua's story of the Wicked Tenants is about his identity. He comes as a prophet and will be killed like one. But the story says more. The prophets were until John the Baptist. But Yeshua identifies himself as something more. He is not like the other servants the vineyard owner sent. At the beginning of his career, Yeshua's status was revealed by John, the last prophet to be something more (Wright, *Jesus and the Victory of God*, 497). Now at the end, Yeshua says it himself. He is no mere prophet. He is the son whom the tenants will kill.

New Tenants

If the vineyard is Israel, the tenant-farmers are the leaders who repeatedly clash with Yeshua. Each one of the gospels develops the story along similar lines. Yeshua becomes a threat early though he does not start any kind of revolt. The leaders watch him and are increasingly hostile. Eventually Yeshua enters their domain and throws down his own challenge, even taking on the greatest symbol of power in Israel, the system of business at the Temple.

But Yeshua is neither anti-Temple nor anti-Israel. His clash is with leaders who are not bringing fruit from the vineyard. And these leaders are mere tenants, not the owners. Yeshua's story undercuts their authority. They rent this land from God and do not own it. The rent is due and they are coming up short.

Yeshua's cutting critique is true to the Hebrew Bible. The land is God's and Israel lives on it at his pleasure. The land will evict them if they do not remain faithful (Lev 18:26-30). The vineyard owner is not a chief priest or a council and is especially not Rome.

So the vineyard will be entrusted to others. Who might Yeshua be referring to? The closest answer at hand is the twelve. Yeshua has said to them that they would sit on twelve thrones and judge the twelve tribes of Israel (Matt 19:28; Luke 22:30). As Luke Johnson notes, this leadership of the twelve over the tribes of Israel will become a theme in the book of Acts (309).

The Son and the Stone

So how do we get from a story about a son who is killed by wicked tenant-farmers to a stone rejected by builders? Yeshua adds a postscript to his story, an application of a scripture from the Hebrew Bible. The rejected son of the vineyard owner leads to a saying about a stone. The connection is closer than it might appear in English, since son is *ben* and stone is *even* (Collins, 543, v and b in Hebrew are the same letter).

In Mark's version, the citation is from Psalm 118:22-23 (which is 117:22-23 in the LXX, from which the citation matches exactly, cf. Johnson, 309). Luke adds Isaiah 8:14, that the stone rejected by the builders will become a stone of stumbling for them, a trap and a snare for Jerusalem.

The Wicked Tenants parable is not about the son's atoning death, but about the condemnation that will come upon those who kill the vineyard owner's son. The house referred to in Psalm 118 is the Temple. The builders of the house are the leaders of Israel, who run the Temple. The rejected stone in Psalm 118 is probably understood as God, but it is well-applied in the new context which Yeshua gives to it. Now, he is saying, the rejected stone is the son whom they are going to kill. And this will be Jerusalem's stumbling stone.

The death of Yeshua is not salvation for all in Israel. For some it is a final act of doom. Yet the vineyard will be given to others, the newly constituted leaders of Israel, the twelve who have followed Yeshua and who will understand all of this later, after the resurrection.

Yeshua is more than a prophet and the movement he leaves is more than a band of disciples. Yeshua is not only the son, in this telling of the story, but the beloved son. It is the same thing the heavenly voice said about Yeshua at the baptism (Mark 1:11; Matt 3:17; Luke 3:22).

Chapter 13

Born from Above
John 3:1-21

Once in a while, not often enough, passages in the Bible transport us into heavenly vistas. This happens not only in some biblical passages, but also in later Jewish literature and Christian literature. We generally call this kind of writing mysticism. The divine realm breaks into the world below with mysteries from above.

These glimpses have generally been unsatisfying, leaving the reader wanting more, inviting further imaginative commentary by later generations. In the history of Judaism mystical literature developed in several streams: the *heichalot* or heavenly palaces, the *merkavah* or divine chariot, *kabbalah*, and *chassidus*. Christianity similarly developed mystical writings and schools, inspired by some Jewish writings and even some New Testament passages (e.g., 2 Cor 12).

One of the early examples of biblical mysticism is the story of Moses and the elders of Israel seeing God walk on a pavement of blue stone and dining with him. Israel's prophets had partial visions of the divine throne with the chief example being Ezekiel's vision of the divine chariot and the holy beings. In apocalyptic writings of the Second Temple period we find a vision of the heavenly palace resplendent in white marble and powerful lightning (1 Enoch 15). Paul speaks obliquely about his own experience of being caught up into the third heaven and seeing visions beyond human comprehension.

With all of this background, are we surprised to find that the fourth gospel, John, is the mystical gospel? Paul Philip Levertoff says of the fourth gospel that it is "the most 'Chasidic' writing in the New Testament" (*Love in the Messianic Age*, 74). Consider some of the mystical ideas presented over and over again in the fourth gospel:

- Heavenly things—the love of God concentrated in the Son—descend to earth and bring union between people and the life that is above.

- Love from eternity past, unknowable in its fulness, moves from the Father to the Son to the world and then back from the world to glorify the Father.

- Birth from above is necessary, a God-initiated renewal of a person's spirit which has its beginning now but will be fully realized in the age to come.

- The divine plan for Yeshua to be lifted up is counter to all human reasoning but is necessary for the presence of Yeshua on earth to permeate the community of faith and change the world.

The connection between God and Yeshua and the world is mysterious, consisting of higher realities than we can comprehend. Yeshua's words in John hint at inexpressible things, a separation between the infinite God and finite humanity that requires supernatural power to bridge.

Typical views of God are too low. In calling children to himself, God has sometimes made the gap seem passable and has manifested his Presence in fire-clouds, angelic appearances, heavenly voices, and in Spirit-empowered prophets. These things led many in Israel to think that mere birth as an Israelite was enough to be assured of rightness with God now and in the world to come. The way to God seemed easy and at hand, since his appearances to the people in various levels of glory was so close, so immediate.

Yet when the divide between light and darkness, the realm below and above, is viewed more precisely, it turns out to be an infinitely distant gap. No human journey can traverse it. The nearness has not been humanity rising up, but divinity reaching down. The glory appearances have not indicated that humanity was close to the heavenly realm, but that God's arm is long in reaching down to pull us up. Yet the end goal is humanity raised up and that requires something new and powerful, a different kind of life, a rebirth, the Spirit given from the Father to the Son and then given from the Son to us.

Nicodemus, as Yeshua said, should have been able as a teacher of Israel to understand at least some of these things. He should have known of the water and Spirit. But he could not possibly understand how it would all work. Yeshua in this discourse rebuffs the inadequate faith of this leading Pharisee, challenging him to look deeper, and hinting at a lifting up which will be necessary to make it all happen—a reference to Yeshua lifted up on a cross, up from the tomb, and up to the heavenly throne. Only later would it be possible for Nicodemus or anyone to understand the full import of Yeshua's words. He was sent from above and the only one who could make the way for us to ascend from worldly life to the life of the age to come.

Teacher from God?

The Nicodemus story is part of a pattern, an illustration of a kind of faith Yeshua regarded as insufficient. The story indicates this by beginning with a conjunctive phrase, "now there was." The now refers the reader back to what was just said in 2:23-25. While in Jerusalem for Passover, many witnessed signs performed by Yeshua. They believed. But Yeshua did not trust their belief. It was insufficient.

Nicodemus is an instance of this larger phenomenon. He also refers to signs that Yeshua performs. The signs he holds up as evidence of the legitimacy of Yeshua in the way that Nicodemus sees Yeshua. And Yeshua does not trust Nicodemus' faith. He finds it insufficient.

"Rabbi," Nicodemus says, "my great one" or perhaps simply "teacher," a form of address intending respect. Occasionally someone addresses Yeshua with sarcasm, but it is not necessary to read sarcasm here. "We know," Nicodemus speaks as if representing some group. He cannot mean, or not in seriousness "we Pharisees." Perhaps the we refers to a group on the council or a group of Nicodemus' peers.

Or perhaps Nicodemus does not realize that his peers will reject Yeshua. After all, we do see him later defending Yeshua (7:51).

"We know that you are a teacher from God." This expression of Yeshua's identity likely means no more than "a teacher approved by God." Yeshua will indicate later in this conversation that he is from above, sent from heaven, and Nicodemus will not understand this. "No one could do signs such as you do unless God was with him." It was the signs that attracted Nicodemus. Raymond Brown suggests that perhaps Nicodemus thought of him as a rabbi for whom God would work wonders (*The Gospel According to John I-XII*, 137). Or he may even have been open to the idea of Yeshua as a Messiah-figure, a scion of the house of David who could be the one. Even so, this was not enough for Yeshua.

The fourth gospel indicates that Yeshua is looking for a deeper faith, a better realization of his identity than simply as a miraculous leader of a Jewish revolt. Yeshua is looking for a fuller realization even than Son of David or Messiah or Son of God as understood in its usual sense. Yeshua is life, the life that is the true light in the darkness, which cannot be overcome (1:4-5, 9). Coming to him in faith is ultimately something requiring God's initiative (1:13; 3:3; 6:44). Those who come to Yeshua don't simply awaken within themselves faith, nor do the reason it out for themselves from the scriptures. They are given to Yeshua by God (5:21; 6:37, 39, 63; 10:29). They receive a special revelation that is mysterious, the voice of the Shepherd, the voice of the Father speaking through Yeshua (7:16-17; 10:27). Yeshua did not utterly reject the kind of faith that came from signs and was about national restoration. He said that his works testified to who he was and he accepted the label Messiah (10:25). Yet he called for a deeper knowledge.

The fourth gospel also indicates that Yeshua understood the gulf between people and God as vast. Bridging the gulf is impossible. The world is in darkness and in need of true light, which comes only in Yeshua (1:4-5, 9). God is unseeable and unknowable (1:18). No one has fully revealed the depths of God until Yeshua. In him was the light that is life for people. No one has descended from heaven but the Son of Man (3:13). No one can give life but the Father and the Father has appointed Yeshua to give this life (5:21, 26-27; 6:27, 33, 63; 10:28; 17:2-3). It is not that the revelation of God up till Yeshua has been for nothing. But it is insufficient. Torah and prophets are not complete until Yeshua's appearance which reveals the Father. Light and life come only when the Son is lifted up. Yeshua brings the promise that we can be born from above.

Birth from Above

Nicodemus comes at night. In a gospel full of imagery of light and darkness we should imagine that this detail is significant. Nicodemus, like the world, is in darkness. But he is coming to the light by coming to Yeshua. The detail may also signify a fear of other Jewish leaders (see 19:38). The whole conversation between Yeshua and Nicodemus will be as between one in darkness and one who is the light that gives life to people.

Yeshua's response to Nicodemus seems odd. The prominent Pharisee has offered Yeshua a word of respect. Rather than receive it, Yeshua seems to take Nicodemus' approach toward him "as an implicit request about entrance into the kingdom of God" (Brown, 138). Yeshua's response ignores and dismisses the words of affirmation from this Pharisee. Yeshua assumes the role of teacher and subordinates Nicodemus, who seems to go along with this. That a Galilean holy man without qualification in the usual sense of Jewish teachers should be so heeded by a man like Nicodemus is a wonder in itself.

Perhaps, Brown suggests, that since everything Yeshua talked about centered on the kingdom, in coming to Yeshua it was apparent that Nicodemus wanted to know about it (138). The usual phrase in the fourth gospel is eternal life in place of kingdom of God. Eternal life means the life of the age to come, the life of the eons. So the fourth gospel makes it central also, simply preferring a different name for it.

"Unless a man is born from above," says Yeshua. Born from above has often been understood as "born again." The word as used in Greek can mean either. That it means born from above is clarified in 3:6. The idea of rebirth can refer to any transformation a person undergoes, but a rebirth from heaven is more than simply remaking ourselves. To be born from above is not simply a rebirth, but a heavenly birth. Nicodemus does not see how this is possible and misunderstands. He assumes this will mean repeating the birth process, which cannot be done.

"Unless a man is born from above he cannot enter the kingdom of God." The fourth gospel here uses the usual phrase from the other gospels "kingdom of God." Perhaps it is the context, a close discussion with a Pharisee, which brings out the more traditional phrase instead of John's preferred term, eternal life.

If Yeshua understands Nicodemus' approach as a cry for help, the openness of a proud man to be taught by someone he recognizes as greater, then Yeshua's answer draws him in even more. Until Nicodemus is ready to let Yeshua explain the meaning of God, of the kingdom, he cannot enter it. Yeshua does not go easy on him. He expects much of this teacher of Israel and will challenge him throughout.

Nicodemus responds with honesty. He can't go back into his mother's womb, can he? He can't become a babe again, can he? What does Yeshua expect of him? Isn't it enough that he, a powerful man, has come to Yeshua with hope in his eyes? But Yeshua speaks in riddles. If the only way into the kingdom is a birth from heaven, then who can enter?

Water and Spirit

Having established, as Raymond Brown puts it "the fact of begetting from on high," Yeshua now turns to explaining "the how of begetting" (136). Perhaps to those practicing Judaism, including a Pharisee like Nicodemus, it seemed easy. We all will enter the kingdom of God, he may have thought. Only sectarians like the Essenes and other apocalyptic orders believed in some greater need than being sons and daughters of Abraham. Being the people of the covenant and Torah, isn't that enough? Being born an Israelite should assure rightness with God, right? Is the way to God so hard?

But the very tradition of Israel Nicodemus sought to be faithful to contained hints of a higher requirement, an act of God in the last times that would prepare people for the life of eternal dwellings. It is a theme started by Moses himself, in the great prophecy of Deuteronomy 30, and continues popping up in a number of places in the prophets:

- The Lord your God will circumcise your heart . . . you will love the Lord your God with all your heart . . . that you may live (Deut 30:6, RSV).

- The palace will be forsaken, the populous city deserted . . . until the Spirit [or simply a spirit] is poured upon us from on high (Isa 32:15, RSV).

- After all of this I will pour out my Spirit on all kinds of people (Joel 3:1-2 or 2:28-29 in Christian Bibles).

- I will put my law within them and write it on their hearts and minds (Jer 31:33).

- I will sprinkle clean water upon you, and you shall be clean from all your uncleannesses . . . And I will put my spirit within you, and cause you to walk in my statutes (Ezek 36:25-27, RSV).

This last reference in Ezekiel is most instructive. We might compare Yeshua words to Nicodemus about the way God begets new life in us with Ezekiel's foretelling of a great outpouring in the last days:

- I will sprinkle clean water upon you, and you shall be clean from all your uncleannesses . . . And I will put my spirit within you, and cause you to walk in my statutes (Ezek 36:25-27, RSV).

- Unless one is born of water and the Spirit, he cannot enter the kingdom of God (John 3:5, RSV).

The image of water brings to mind the purification of impurity, which usually happened through bathing or immersion in the Torah. But in one case, corpse impurity, there was a sprinkling with water (Num 19:11-13). Ezekiel's image and also Yeshua's is of a person in their guilt being made clean with a divine cleansing with water. This is followed by a union between God's spirit (the Holy Spirit) and people, which is a rather mystical connection between God and people.

So, what is Yeshua saying? Is he saying that these great events of the last days must happen now if people are to enter the kingdom of God (or as the fourth gospel would usually put it, have eternal life)?

In all the gospels there is a tension between now and not yet. The promises in Ezekiel and other prophets are for the great time in the future, the not yet. But Yeshua has said the kingdom is near and eternal life is for now, not just then. As with other cases of now and not yet, we should probably read Yeshua's meaning as a partial realization now of something yet to come in its fullness. It may be in the last days that people will become guilt-free, pure, and endued with the Spirit of God in perfect union so that their love and righteousness will be complete. But Yeshua says that something like that must also happen now.

Yeshua says it is mysterious, mystical, this union between God and people that must happen now. The Spirit is like the wind (and the same word means spirit in both Greek and Hebrew). It's voice or sound (again, same word) is heard, but it cannot be seen and its origin is unknown. The union between God and people is already happening. Yeshua is going to make it happen. And he will do so by being lifted up.

The Son Lifted Up

Nicodemus asks a third question, "How can these things be?" Yeshua implies that a teacher in Israel like Nicodemus should understand (vs. 10). Yeshua has told Nicodemus of earthly things—that begetting from above is required to enter the kingdom—but Nicodemus' circle has not believed this. The Jewish leaders are not on a quest to deepen union with God through faith. They are on a quest for political power, some seeking revolution against Rome, others maintaining power over Temple and religious law.

Now Yeshua is going to tell Nicodemus something heavenly, something of divine origin which will not make sense to earthly ears. Yeshua proceeds to tell him in three parts:

1. Only one has descended from heaven, and thus has ascended, who is the Son of Man.

2. This Son of Man must be lifted up, like the copper snake in Numbers 21.

3. Those who see and believe in this lifting up of the Son of Man have eternal life.

Yeshua's first point derives from the view of God in the fourth gospel: no one has seen God (1:18). One could easily object: what about Moses or the Israelites who saw the glory cloud? Yeshua says only he has ascended to heaven. One could easily object: what about Enoch or Elijah?

The fourth gospel has a high view of God. Moses and the Israelites did not see God as he is in himself, but manifestations of his presence. The Presence, the Glory, the Name, the Word, the *Shechinah*—these are all emanations of God's glory, but not God in his direct being. Some have ascended to heaven, but not in the fullest sense, not into the innermost circle in direct union with God. Only Yeshua, the Son of Man, was in heaven in this full sense.

Why does Yeshua speak of his ascension in the past tense? Isn't it true that he won't ascend until after the resurrection? There is some lack of clarity here on Yeshua's intention. It may be that since Yeshua was in heaven, in direct union with the Father from eternity past (17:24), he can speak of ascension as a past-tense-realized fact. It may be that the resurrection and ascension which are still future are so certain, they can be spoken of in a prophetic past (sometimes the prophets use the past tense for something God has yet to do). In any case, Yeshua alone has been in direct union with the Father and Yeshua alone possesses the knowledge of the Father's plan.

The Father's plan is nonsense to earthly ears. To bring the life of eternity to people, the Son of Man must be lifted up—up on a cross, up from the tomb, and up to the right hand of God on the heavenly throne. Yeshua likens this to the story in Numbers 21:4-9 about a snake of copper (or bronze) which Moses had made to be lifted up on a pole. The Israelites looked to the image of the snake and were healed. The Aramaic paraphrases of Yeshua's day, the Targums, said about this story that the Israelites looked for healing to the *Memra* of God, the Word of God, the manifestation of God on earth (Brown, 133). This is exactly who Yeshua is claiming to be: the one with all the nature of God manifested on earth, the radiation of God's being, his Word or Presence. In *kabbalistic* terminology (from later Judaism), Yeshua is the sum of all the *sefirot* (emanations) and the Father is the *Ein Sof* (the One without End, the unseeable One, see 1:18). In the language of Hebrews 1:3, Yeshua is "the radiance of his glory and the representation of his essence."

But as surprising as it may be that the Father has sent his Presence (Yeshua), it is more surprising that the destiny of the Presence is to be lifted up on a Roman cross. However, this lifting up will be also from the tomb (resurrection) and to the heavenly throne (ascension). As Yeshua said elsewhere: "When you lift up the Son of Man, then you will know that I am" (John 8:28). This truth is heavenly, unknowable and unforeseeable to earthly minds. It is a plan that can only come from the Father, the one who loved the world enough to give up his Son (3:16).

And as those who looked to the copper snakes in the desert were healed, so those who believe in Yeshua lifted up "will not perish, but have eternal life" (3:16).

Love and Life

John 3:16 has a reputation as one of the best-known verses in the Bible. In the larger context of John 3:1-21, the meaning of this remarkable verse is only heightened. The identity of the Son and the Father has been emphasized. The Father is the unknowable, utterly transcendent God. The Son is the radiance of his glory, his Word, his *Memra*, his Presence.

"God so loved the world" is a past tense, in Greek an aorist, suggesting one point in time in the past, a "supreme act of love" (Brown, 133). It was before the world was made, in that time the Father and Son shared before creation (17:24). God decided to "give" and also to "give up" the Son. Thus, the Son was born as a man (incarnation) and also the Son was given up to death (the cross).

We are meant to see the disparity: the Son given up for the world, what was most dear to the Father for those who rebelled against him.

So what then of the requirement that people believe? Those who do not are in a sense "condemned already" (3:18), but in another sense the condemnation is not until "the last day" (12:48). The fourth gospel emphasizes both present and future aspects of hope and doom. We are more familiar with the future aspect: all will be judged either for hope or doom on the last day, the day of the Lord. Here in the third chapter, the emphasis is on the present. What we do with Yeshua now matters ultimately. If we believe, we already have the life of the eons. If we disbelieve, we already have the verdict of judgment.

As airtight as this seems, leaving no room for doubt about the final destiny of any person who does not believe, several factors leave much room for hope for all those who currently do not believe in Yeshua:

- Statements of present judgment ("judged already") are balanced by statements of future judgment ("the last day")—so there is still time for people to believe.

- Yeshua's stern warnings should probably be interpreted as regarding those who encountered him on earth, saw his signs, and yet disbelieved.

- God has ways of making himself known that are beyond our understanding and there is always room for hope when it comes to the final destiny of any person.

Yet the point of 3:17-18 is that a person is obliged to believe in God's Son. In one sense this is like the requirement to believe in the prophet God will raise up:

I will raise up for them a prophet like you from among their brethren; and I will put my words in his mouth, and he shall speak to them all that I command him. And whoever will not give heed to my words which he shall speak in my name, I myself will require it of him (Deut 18:18-19, RSV).

And so the coming of the Son, which should be about saving, has a sad note also. The Son came to save and not to condemn. But it is inevitable that some will not open themselves to the kind of life God is giving. Some will shut themselves off from divine life, because they prefer darkness.

Light and Darkness

Vss. 19-20 can be isolated from the rest as a general wisdom saying. Yeshua applies this wisdom saying to the context of the coming of the Son to be lifted up and save the world. The light is truth and life. But evil prefers the shadows. Light shows motivations, reality, it unconceals what has been concealed. And evil does not wish to be exposed, because it is a lie.

This is true in the absolute sense and in the practical sense. In the absolute sense, evil wishes to deceive because in truth evil does not exist. Evil is nothing without good, being merely a perversion of good, just as shadow has no real substance, but is only absence or blocking of light. So evil only looks desirable from the shadows. Shine too much light on evil and the truth is revealed. It becomes nothing but selfish hatred.

In the practical sense, criminals hide in the shadows. In our acts of selfishness we avoid truth-revealing light, because if we examine the reasons we work for anything other than healing and serving and loving we find something ugly and base about ourselves.

Yeshua applied this to the coming of the Son from the Father. Yeshua is the light that gives life to men (1:4-5, 9). Those who prefer darkness run from Yeshua, like the Jewish leaders of his time. Yeshua implied here and elsewhere that his generation's leaders knew he was the light. But they shrank from this vision of hope which came in an unexpected way. They preferred their own ideas about power and messianic hope for the nation. Yeshua's coming causes some to be attracted to the light and some to scurry away from it.

But those who come to the light, who find that the Son is the life and light indeed, are in for a surprise. They find that their deeds have been done in God. That is, they find that God has initiated it all from the beginning. Their birth is from above. Their attraction to the light was God calling. Their acts of love and goodness have been overseen by God. They find that they have been in union with God in ways that are beyond understanding.

Summary

The story of Yeshua and Nicodemus in John 3:1-21 is remarkable and the ideas in this story are repeated in various ways throughout the fourth gospel. The meaning of the story is realizing that God is greater than we thought. He is not simply a physical deliverer, not simply a Presence in the Tabernacle of Israel, not simply the One who gave Torah to Israel on Sinai. He is also the unknowable, mysterious, transcendent One who promised a begetting from above in the last days (Deut 30:6; various prophetic passages). Nicodemus' understanding of God, Torah, and life in the age to come needed a corrective.

Yeshua is not merely a "teacher from God" but the Son who is sent by the Father. And the divine plan is heavenly, not earthly. It is not about revolutions or Sanhedrins. It is about the lifting up of the Son on a cross, from a tomb, and to the heavenly throne. From there he will give the Spirit, the presence of Yeshua on earth (called the *Paraclete* in John 14-16). People will be infused with the life of the eons, union with God, if they believe.

The view of God, of the life to come, and of union with God in John 3 is mystical. Hope in a Messiah born of David's line who brings about a time in history when Israel is restored is only the beginning of faith. The physical hope matters, because God is not the god of the Gnostics who is pure spirit and who disdains physical being. The life of the eons is not anti-physical, just as the resurrected Yeshua in the fourth gospel is not a mere ghost. But the view of the fourth gospel is that the life to come is the physical raised up to the level of spirit, the physical in complete union with God. And this eternal life begins now. It is partially realized already for those who believe. The Son has ascended and his presence is here now, in the Spirit. It is unseen and unprovable, but capable of being grasped by those who would come to the light.

Chapter 14

Messiah's Trial
Mark 14:53-65

The story of Yeshua's trial before the Sanhedrin, the ruling council of Judaism based in Jerusalem, is one that has caused trouble in the intervening centuries since the gospels started circulating. Anyone unfamiliar with the Christian form of anti-Semitism, inspired by an idea that the Jews (all Jews in every generation) killed Jesus, find it easily by reading European history (or Jewish history or honest accounts of church history).

A modern reader of the story of Yeshua's trial cannot avoid associations of this trial with ideas of Judaism and Christianity's antagonism towards each other. So we need to be reminded from the beginning that this was not at all an issue at the time these events happened. The story of Yeshua's trial is an inner-Jewish problem. It is not Jesus-the-Christian being put on trial by the priests-as-Orthodox-Jews. It is rather Yeshua the Jewish troublemaker being put on trial by the Jewish council protecting the status quo with Rome, its own power, and its rule over the Temple.

A modern reader may object to the story of Yeshua's trial for three reasons. First, it is a biased account. Second, it is easily read as anti-Jewish. Third, the story is cryptic—what were these Jewish authorities hoping to prove and what do Yeshua's silences and answers mean?

The trial before the Jewish authorities was not the only one Yeshua faced. He also faced a Roman trial before Pilate (and a brief hearing before Herod Antipas). But our investigation here will concern the Jewish trial in Mark's version (14:53-65). There

113

are a number of details to consider if we compare the accounts in all four gospels, but I will not comment on them. The account in Mark gives a well-rounded perspective on what happened and deserves study on its own.

Before considering the story itself, we should address the concerns that it is biased and potentially anti-Jewish. Those who want to know what Yeshua's life was all about have reason to be concerned. A biased story may give us a distorted view of what he was really about. Why did the Jewish authorities of the time want him dead or is it possible that they did not really condemn him? Does this mean we should read Yeshua more like a Christian and less like a Jew, as one who departed from the faith of his people and started a new faith?

Yeshua, the Rural Religious Fanatic

We ought not be too concerned that the story of Yeshua's trial is biased. As Raymond Brown notes, the motivations of the Jewish council were no doubt mixed, an "admixture of insincerity, self-protective cunning, honest religious devotion, conscientious soul-searching, and fanaticism" (*The Death of the Messiah*, 434). There is plenty of historical evidence for political machination and even violence from the high priests in Israel during this time. And there are evidences of corruption among the chief priests especially from the time period and from later sources looking back.

So, even if the story is biased, even if it is possible that to anyone who was there, the men of the Sanhedrin were doing their best to sincerely protect Israel from Roman persecution, the reading of this trial as one treating Yeshua unfairly is certainly a valid perspective. The best light in which the high priest is portrayed is in John, where he says that if they do not have Yeshua executed the Romans might take away Israel's religious freedom and Temple (John 11:47-50).

Yeshua was dangerous. He was more dangerous for the way he could be misunderstood than for what he actually taught. To the elite of Jerusalem, Yeshua was a rural, religious fanatic. He come from circles outside the accepted cadre of leaders (mostly priests and aristocrats, but also scholars and scribes). He was popular (which always makes someone potentially dangerous). He taught about issues which, understood in their most apocalyptic form, could lead Rome to see a revolutionary in the making.

One of the issues that comes up in the trial is something that Jews of the time fought about internally and also one which later Christians and Jews had strong feelings about: the Temple. Some of Yeshua's actions appeared to be anti-Temple and some of his words also. We will see that Mark dispels the idea that Yeshua was anti-Temple or that he viewed it as obsolete. But there was an earlier example in history of a Jewish prophet who was anti-Temple. And he too was treated violently by the leaders of his generation. That prophet was Jeremiah.

Raymond Brown says of Jeremiah that he is "an outstanding example of the innocent just one made to suffer by the leaders of God's own people" (396). "Change the way you have been living and do what is right" said Jeremiah (7:3) or God will destroy this Temple which gives you false hope that you way of living is right (7:14). Jeremiah was a prophet who challenged the way people viewed the Temple. In modern terms, his message would be, "You religious people are hiding behind religious actions as if those make you right with God."

The priests and prophets (false prophets) of the time did just what the Jewish leadership in Yeshua's time did. They judged Jeremiah worthy of execution (Jer 26:7-11). Jeremiah, like Yeshua, was a "disturbing challenger of the religious structures of his time" (Brown, 396).

The biased account of Yeshua's trial before the Sanhedrin is not some later anti-Jewish Christian propaganda. It reflects the very real motives of a powerful leadership of mixed motives, holding together a loose alliance of interest groups and a volatile political situation with Rome. And Yeshua's responses in the trial were not to save his own life, but were, if anything, intended to ensure his own indictment and handing over to the Romans.

Seeking Evidence of Yeshua as a Temple-Destroyer

Already convinced that Yeshua is dangerous, and having decided long before the trial that he should be put to death, the Sanhedrin is looking for evidence. Most likely they want to gather evidence to present to Pilate to convince him to execute Yeshua.

From the perspective of the chief priests, the Temple is the most important institution in the life of Israel. Economically, the Temple was a major part of the economy. In religious terms, though sectarians like the Essenes avoided the corrupt Temple and though the Pharisees de-emphasized it with new rituals centered in the Jewish home, the Temple was the center of devotion, zeal, and the nearness of the Jewish people to God.

Two things in the career of Yeshua made him suspect as a Temple-opponent. He has been heard talking about it being destroyed and he initiated a protest action in the Temple.

In Mark's telling of the story, talk about the destruction of the Temple has been only in a discourse with his inner circle of disciples: Peter, James, John, and Andrew (13:3). Yeshua said things like "not one stone will be left upon another" (13:2).

In the larger issue of the historical Yeshua and his sayings about the Temple, we know he said more than this. For one thing, even in Mark, it is apparent that Yeshua's enemies hold against him a perceived threat to the Temple: "Aha! You who can destroy the Temple and rebuild it in three days . . ." (15:29).

Perhaps the best historical evidence for this comes in the fourth gospel. It was not right at the end of his career, but nearer the beginning, that the fourth gospel places both a saying about the Temple being destroyed and also Yeshua's protest action against the Temple (John 2:12-22).

The idea in the fourth gospel that Yeshua's protest action, commonly known as cleansing the Temple, came at the beginning of his career is problematic. First, it is reported at the end of his career in the synoptic gospels (Mark 11:15-18; Matt 21:12-13; Luke 19:45-48). Second, the synoptics indicate that his Temple protest was the immediate cause of his arrest (Mark 11:18). Third, it is hard to imagine the Jewish leaders not arresting Yeshua for such a threat to the greatest symbol of their power and the centerpiece of Israelite religion and economy.

Historically, the solution has been proposed by Raymond Brown (and we discussed it earlier in chapter 7). The fourth gospel is right that Yeshua's saying about the Temple and his questioning by Temple authorities happened early. And the fourth gospel chose to report the Temple protest at that time, for its own literary reasons, even though the protest actually happened at the end of his career (Brown, *The Gospel According to John I-XII*, 118). Yeshua, early in his career, got involved in some dispute with Temple authorities that led them to question him. He responded with a curious saying about the Temple being destroyed and rebuilt in three days. Then, late in his career, he drove out the sellers of animals and money-changers in a Temple protest action.

This is why, at his trial, the Sanhedrin cannot find a witness who heard Yeshua speaking of Temple destruction. Yeshua's saying had come much earlier. It was known and was part of his reputation, but witnesses are now hard to find.

But more than the issue of early or late in his career, the issue Mark's telling brings to the fore is that the council found false testimony against Yeshua. What was false about the testimony?

The answer is simple, whether we consider the account from Mark itself or bring in evidence from the fourth gospel. The witnesses, as well as the mockers when Yeshua is on the cross, say that Yeshua spoke himself of destroying the temple: "We heard him say, 'I will destroy this Temple made with hands'" (Mark 14:58). But this is false. Yeshua said the Temple would be destroyed, using the passive voice (Mark 13:2) and in John 2:19 he spoke of the Jewish leaders themselves destroying it. Yeshua never said he would destroy the Temple or that he was against the Temple. He simply foretold that it would be destroyed.

It is important to Mark that Yeshua was killed as an innocent sufferer and not a revolutionary. Yeshua did not confront the power of the chief priests with a military revolution, but with a revolution of ideas. His kingdom is not of this world, not in the sense that the Sanhedrin or Rome thought of worldly power.

Are You Messiah, Son of the Blessed?

Not only is Yeshua a perceived Temple-destroyer, but this rural, religious upstart is even more dangerous, from the Sanhedrin's point of view, as a would-be Messiah. This is the very reason Yeshua has suppressed talk of his Messianic identity (see chapter 6, "The Messianic Secret"). Common ideas of Messiah, both in the official thought of the religious leaders and in various revolutionary movements of the time (documented in Josephus) include violence and leading an insurrection.

Yeshua has already been explicit, in private with his disciples, that he is the Messiah (Mark 8:29-30). The Messianic secret has not been about denying his exalted identity and authority, but in cautiously teaching his inner circles a deeper meaning of the messianic role. Yeshua exceeds in every way the common ideas of Messiah's origin and authority. And Yeshua's mission is not crass revolution, but the renewal of Israel through his own suffering and exaltation (resurrection and ascension). Yeshua did not come to conquer, but to be killed. And it is about to happen.

Yeshua assured his death when the high priest asked, "Have you no answer?" Yeshua was silent. His silence should be read as deliberate, not as if he was at a loss for words. Yeshua will not defend himself.

This leads the high priest to the issue of blasphemy. Is Yeshua the Temple-critic also a crazed fanatic believing himself to be Israel's king or even semi-divine?

Yeshua's answer is, "I am." Matthew and Luke give a more complex answer, which sounds like a qualified affirmation. Raymond Brown demonstrates that even in Matthew and Luke Yeshua is not denying, but owning the titles put to him (*The Death of the Messiah*, 488-93). Mark skips the complexity, which can be confusing, and gets right to the point. Yeshua agrees that he is both Messiah and Son of God.

The title "Son of the Blessed One" or "Son of God" is usually understood as a Messianic title. The Davidic king is God's son (2 Sam 7:14; Psa 2:7). But the high priest likely has seen something more potentially blasphemous in Yeshua's use of the term. While Yeshua has avoided calling himself Son of God (preferring Son of Man), he has spoken many times of his father, indicating that God is his father. This kind of talk exceeds even normal messianic thought. It possibly sounded to the ears of Jewish leaders like some Greek or Roman idea of demigods or like some strange Jewish sectarian belief. It is tantamount to claiming divinity.

Yeshua does not shirk from the implications of the question. He affirms all of these ideas. No statement of his exalted status and identity could be too high for him to deny. The high priest did not miss this implication, but tore his clothes and judged Yeshua a blasphemer on the spot.

Yeshua's Son of Man Saying

Yeshua's use of the title Son of Man has been a coded way of describing his identity and authority. The title itself can be simply a term for a man. But in the context of talk about the kingdom and in the environment of Yeshua's lofty descriptions of his role and power, it almost certainly has meant to the crowds the Son of Man in Daniel 7. To one like a Son of Man the Ancient of Days has given a kingdom that lasts forever. And the Son of Man has authority over all peoples, Israel and the nations.

Always creative in his way of using old symbols and investing them with new meaning, Yeshua has used the Son of Man talk in surprising and creative ways. Just as Yeshua's idea of the mission of Messiah has not been the standard view of his time, Yeshua has said repeatedly that the Son of Man must suffer, has no place, and will be delivered to the Jewish authorities to die. On the other side, he has said that the Son of Man is lord of the Sabbath, will judge Israel in the last days, and has authority on earth to forgive sins.

Yeshua creatively combines the lofty identity of the Son of Man with a Son of Man whose mission it is to suffer redemptively.

Now, though the high priest has asked about the titles Messiah and Son of the Blessed One, Yeshua brings the language back to his preferred term. He says two things about the Son of Man, both of which are vital to understanding how Yeshua saw his mission:

- You will see the Son of Man sitting at the right hand of Power [God]

- You will see the Son of Man coming with the clouds of heaven.

There are two questions that spring from these sayings: (1) what does Yeshua mean about the sitting and the coming and (2) what does he mean that they, the Sanhedrin, will see these things?

There are many complex arguments to the effect that Yeshua's Son of Man saying at his trial refers only to the events which came forty years later, the destruction of the Temple. In other words, Yeshua was not talking about anything which would come in the far future (his return at the end of the age), but only things in the near term (the destruction of the Temple).

In this view, when the Romans came and slaughtered the Jewish leaders along with many of the people and leveled the Temple and most of Jerusalem, this is to be equated with the Son of Man sitting at the right hand of Power and coming with the clouds (Wright, *Jesus and the Victory of God*, 524-5).

Raymond Brown cuts through this mistaken interpretation of Mark 14:62 with two points:

- "... Mark means us to think of a sequence from one action to the other, for obviously one cannot sit and come at the same time" (*The Death of the Messiah*, 497).

- Mark's saying "you will see" must mean something sooner than forty years later (498-500).

The gospels, especially the fourth, but also the synoptics, affirm both present realization of the age to come and future realization throughout. The promises ultimately are for the future but have partial realization now. The kingdom is now and not yet.

In the ultimate sense, the Son of Man's sitting at the right hand of Power (from Psa 110:1) happens at the ascension. The coming of the Son of Man with the clouds is a separate event, the return of Messiah at the end of the age (cast in the language of Dan 7:13) to receive the kingdom. It is true, as N.T. Wright asserts, that in Daniel this coming with the clouds is not to earth, but to the throne of God. But Yeshua reuses the statements of the Hebrew Bible creatively and we should not press such details too closely.

And there is plenty in Yeshua's teaching that speaks of the delay of the kingdom. The idea that Yeshua expected to return in a very short time after the cross is hard to argue in light of many statements of delay, not least Mark 13:32. There Yeshua, though speaking of the destruction of the Temple and the coming events of the last days, says he does not know when the time will be.

So, if, as the two actions in Yeshua's Son of Man saying seem to suggest, the reference is to Yeshua's ascension (sitting) and return (coming), then what does he mean "you will see"?

The Jewish leaders will see it when, at the death of Yeshua, the veil in the Temple is torn (Mark 15:38). They will see it when the tomb is empty and when they hear reports that Yeshua is alive and eventually that he has ascended. The Romans see it, representatively at least through one man, a centurion, who witnesses Yeshua's death and decides this man truly was the Son of God (Mark 15:39). Raymond Brown suggests these are the kind of things Yeshua meant by "you will see" and says that it should have been apparent that the death of Yeshua was extraordinary, though it was still possible for Jewish and Roman leaders to explain these things away (500).

Blasphemy and the Threat in Yeshua's Words

The Sanhedrin did not have trouble seeing in Yeshua's statement about the Son of Man, which they likely understood as a figure he used for himself, a threat. Not only did Yeshua answer affirmatively that he was the Messiah, Son of the Blessed, but he dared to suggest that his authority and coming into power would be seen by the council.

The high priest's reaction was to tear his clothes, a sign of grief. In this case, it was grief over hearing blasphemy in Israel. Brown gives evidence of the ancient practice amongst Romans and Israelites of tearing clothes upon receiving bad news, even other than someone's death (517-9).

The council's reaction was to determine he was worthy of death. They did not act upon this themselves (the reasons may have been complex, but no doubt involved a desire not to anger Pilate). Their verdict meant they would bring Yeshua before the Romans to be executed.

And they blindfolded Yeshua, this rural, religious upstart who dared in front of the council to give himself exalted, messianic status and to threaten divine judgment. Yeshua's answer implied that he held greater religious authority than the Sanhedrin itself. From their point of view he was a self-deluded would-be prophet and messiah. So they mocked him by calling on him to prophesy something.

Yeshua, referring to himself as the Son of Man, passed judgment on his judges. He did not try to save his life. It was the mission of the Son of Man to suffer and to die redemptively. Once he had threatened and offended the Sanhedrin, the end was near.

It is not difficult to see why Yeshua would be sentenced by a Jewish court of his day. His teachings often cut against the opinions of the chief priests and of the scribes. His statements about himself were so lofty they were easily seen as blasphemous. Though he performed miracles, they were not of the sort expected for a messianic figure (they did not lead to independence from Rome). He was not anything the people were looking for as a Messiah, much less the leaders. Even the disciples did not understand his death. Who was this Son of Man who came to die and not to conquer?

Chapter 15

Crucifixion Irony
Mark 15:16-39

Mark's account of Yeshua's death is punctuated with irony. The story of the innocent sufferer in the Hebrew Bible is interlaced with the agony and incongruity of the punishment of the Son of God. The sky darkens with God's anger, not least his anger directed against his own Son, suffering for his nation and his disciples, drawing on himself the anger of God and bringing the time of woes into reality. That Yeshua's path to the Roman cross has been deliberate is obvious. That he faces it determined but with the cracks of human weakness is mysterious. That victory should look like this is unspeakable.

Unlike the many statements leading up to the crucifixion, the story of how it happened itself is concerned less with theology than with presenting in stark reality the betrayal of a good man, the senseless mockery, the brutal misunderstanding of what his kingdom is all about. Meaning is between the lines, a *midrashic* retelling of the innocent sufferer theme in the Hebrew Bible. *Midrash* is a Jewish world of thought based on scriptural texts. The texts used in *midrashic* retelling need not be interpreted according to context, but reflect theology and ideas from outside of the texts themselves. Connections between different places in the Bible are often found. In the case of the story of Yeshua's death, many different texts about the innocent sufferer are used. So even details like soldiers gambling for Yeshua's clothes are connected to ancient words about an innocent sufferer's indignation. Yeshua suffers like the just men who were persecuted in the pages of the Hebrew Bible.

123

Behind the irony of the story is the community of Yeshua's followers at the time the story was committed to writing. The ideology behind the story is one of exaltation, Yeshua is believed to be the king at God's right hand. But the Son of Man to whom the kingship of Israel and the nations belongs is the Son of Man who is handed over to the chief priests and soldiers to be mishandled and killed. The story occurs with the understanding that the man so abused is greater than any observers realize, including the disciples themselves at the time. The unit ends with supreme irony. The Roman supervisor of this travesty understands what no one at the time does. This man is the king.

The Mockery

Pilate maintained a home in Jerusalem as well as Caesarea. There is a tradition that this home was in the Antonia fortress, but it is more likely a home lost to time, the more lavish palace of Herod the Great from an earlier era in Jerusalem (Brown, *The Death of the Messiah*, 706-10). The cohort that was called up may have been 500 or more troops. Perhaps Pilate did this in case the death of Yeshua caused trouble in the city. Pilate regularly maintained a full cohort in the city in case of riots (Collins, 725).

The parading of Yeshua in a mock robe with a fake scepter is a Roman tradition in triumphal parades of prisoners. The mocked person would be hailed as Caesar. History records many similar examples (Evans and Wright, 27).

The irony of Mark's messianic secret theme (see chapter 6) is now fully realized. When misunderstood and crassly presented, Yeshua's kingship is a matter for the Roman provincial government to mock. What can a man and a few disciples do to Rome?

For Mark's audience the irony was already apparent. Yeshua was already believed by hundreds of thousands in a movement across the empire to be more of a king than Caesar. The watchword of the Yeshua community was "Yeshua is Lord," a deliberate challenge to Caesar's honor.

If these soldiers knew how history would advance they would realize Yeshua actually would conquer Rome and that they were helping to make it happen. It would not be a conquest of the type they would imagine but even more real and lasting. A day would come when Caesar was only a memory. But Yeshua is revered still.

The simplistic understanding of Messiah is much like the Roman understanding of Yeshua's potential as a revolutionary. Movements of military resistance leave their mark on history and then pass. But the king of the Jewish people is more than a human conqueror or the bringer of a golden age in Jerusalem. No wonder Yeshua sought to keep his kingship muted while teaching his inner circle to be open to revelations of something much greater. Simplistic messiahs like those who rose up before and after Yeshua come and go. The world is not looking ultimately for Caesar or Bar Kochba.

Simon Carries the Cross

It is a matter of curiosity that the story in Mark (also Matthew and Luke) mentions that Yeshua's cross was carried part of the way by a Jewish pilgrim in town for the Passover, one Simon the Cyrene. Cyrene was a Greek colony in North Africa known to have a Jewish community (Collins, 735-6).

There are two reasons likely for this part of the story being remembered. First, it is an example of something Yeshua taught his disciples: ""If anyone wants to become my follower, he must deny himself, take up his cross, and follow me" (Mark 8:34). Second, it appears that some of Mark's readers might possibly know Simon's two sons, Alexander and Rufus (Collins, 736). Though they are not mentioned again in the New Testament, the way their names are dropped suggests familiarity.

Golgotha

The location of the place Yeshua was crucified is a matter of opinion and guesswork to some degree. Modern pilgrims to Jerusalem have two spots vying for the honor at Gordon's Calvary and the Holy Sepulchre church. The Holy Sepulchre church is likely closer if not the actual spot. Collins prefers a suggestion of a spot two hundred meters south of the Holy Sepulchre (740).

Golgotha is an Aramaic place name related to the word skull. The reason for the name is unknown. Many today know it by a derivation of its Latin name, Calvary (from *calvaria* or skull).

Wine with Myrrh

Was the spiced wine a drug? A luxury? Or a cruel, bitter offering intended to further frustrate the thirsty, dying man? A lot has been written. It is unlikely that myrrh was thought to be a strong narcotic, but there is a later tradition that women of Jerusalem would offer a sedative of wine and myrrh to victims of the Romans. Others see it as spiced wine, a luxury, which has its own evidence in ancient texts. But it could possibly also be a cruel offer of an unpalatably bitter, strong draught of myrrh (a bitter resin sought for aroma and not taste, see Collins 740-4 for the whole discussion).

Matthew's account connects the offering of spiced wine with Psalm 69:22(21), "They give me gall for food, vinegar to quench my thirst" (Matt 27:34). Mark does not take the opportunity to use this connection to the innocent sufferer theme. But in mentioning it, and if it was a sort of gall as Matthew interprets it, Mark is again emphasizing the cruelty. In death and bleeding, Yeshua is no doubt desperately thirsty.

Gambling Over Garments

The property of an executed criminal was forfeited to the authorities (Evans and Wright, 32). Mark, unlike John, does not develop any potential symbolism about Yeshua's garments. He only develops the theme of the innocent sufferer from this incident.

Psalm 22 is the quintessential voice of the innocent sufferer which has many comparisons to the crucifixion of Yeshua. Mark does not use Psalm 22, as some later Christian writers, as a messianic prophecy, but instead for its themes and its hints of a victory after suffering.

Mark 15:24 is a strong allusion to Psalm 22:19(18). The wording in Mark is nearly identical to the Psalm with the person changed to third. This will be one of several echoes from Psalm 22.

Third Hour

On a sundial, the third hour is approximately nine o'clock in the morning (noon is the sixth hour). There is a discrepancy with John 19:14. Whether this discrepancy can be harmonized is uncertain. Historically speaking, the mention of a time in Mark's account seems to have no purpose other than passing on the information delivered about how the event happened. It is one of many signs that Mark's account is using earlier sources to report actual events.

The Inscription, "King of the Jews"

The travesty of Yeshua's royal identity juxtaposed with his cruel treatment is further highlighted by the title or charge nailed to his cross. There are references in historical sources to the charges against Roman victims being posted at their crucifixion (Evans and Wright, 31).

For Mark the details of Pilate's motives in having this *titulus* or placard placed on Yeshua's cross are not important. It is again the irony, that the Jewish leaders have truly handed over the king to Rome, and that the mocking Romans really are crucifying the once and for all king of Israel.

Two Thieves

There is little reason for the notice of the two thieves except to hint at another *midrashic* connection between Yeshua and the innocent sufferer of the Hebrew Bible. Isaiah 53:12 speaks of the sufferer (figuratively Israel in Isaiah but also one who stands in for Israel, i.e., Messiah) who is "numbered with the transgressors." Luke 22:37 makes this connection directly, citing Isaiah 53:12. In some late manuscripts of Mark there is a verse 28 inserted (missing in modern versions) to also make this connection (but this was not original to the gospel, but added later).

Mark's ironic account continues. Yeshua, the man whose goodness and benevolence surpass anyone, is crucified between two criminals. The innocent sufferer is regarded by onlookers (and by God, as will be hinted later) as bearing guilt.

They Shook Their Heads

The shaking of heads is possibly an allusion to Lamentations 2:15, where observers of Jerusalem's destruction and indignity "sneered and shook their heads." Jerusalem was not exactly an innocent sufferer like Yeshua, but there was in the mockery of Jerusalem injustice and misunderstanding. God judged his city, but still loved it. So God was judging Yeshua here, but still loving him.

These mockers who are unidentified have heard the rumor that Yeshua is some kind of anti-Temple prophet (see chapter 14). This is a false rumor, as Mark has told us. Of the four gospels, only John records Yeshua's saying that the Temple would be rebuilt in three days (John 2:20), but Yeshua neither said he would destroy the Temple nor spoke of a literal rebuilding in three days. The reference was a cryptic one to his resurrection.

Again Mark is emphasizing the innocence of Yeshua. Those who despise him base their hatred on false ideas about what Yeshua has said. The guilt he bears is not his own, but theirs.

Mockery by Chief Priests

Those who sentenced Yeshua and brought him to Pilate had heard Yeshua say he was the Messiah, Son the Blessed One and also to imply that he was the Son of Man who would sit at God's right hand and come with power (Mark 14:61-62). They had blindfolded him and challenged him to prophesy (Mark 14:65).

Now, continuing the irony of the scene, they offer to see and believe, the very things Yeshua has been teaching people to do, if he will show them one more sign. The sign they demand is that he save himself.

The irony is multiple, because Yeshua is saving Israel as they watch, but they ignorantly mock his role as a savior. Yeshua saves others by not saving himself. It is the crucial belief of the Yeshua community: his death is a ransom (Mark 10:45). Yeshua submitted to this in the Garden the night he was arrested (Mark 14:36) and by not defending himself at his trial (Mark 14:61). The servant humbles himself to the point of death and in so doing saves (see Phil 2:8). The reader is not supposed to miss the fact that Yeshua's mockers speak unwitting truth.

Darkness at Noon

Mark is possibly alluding to another them in the Hebrew Bible here, Amos 8:9, which is not about the innocent sufferer. Amos was speaking about the coming judgment against the northern tribes of Israel. He said that the day of judgment would be terrible: "'In that day,' says the sovereign Lord, 'I will make the sun set at noon and make the earth dark in the middle of the day.'"

Why is the sky darkened from noon until Yeshua death sometime around three o'clock in Mark's story. The idea that God is angry is clear. Is this anger directed at Yeshua or Jerusalem? Is Yeshua taking the punishment of Israel on himself or is Israel making punishment for itself since its leaders condemned Yeshua? Mark's answer will be hinted at in the dying cry of Yeshua (see below).

Eloi and Eliyahu

Psalm 22, the quintessential Psalm of the innocent sufferer, is not just a text which Mark found useful in framing Yeshua's death. It is a text Yeshua quoted from the cross. Psalm 22:1, "My God, my God, why have you abandoned me?" is the source of Yeshua's saying.

Much has been written about shades of meaning in Yeshua quoting Psalm 22. Some think Yeshua feels abandoned because he expected to see salvation while on the cross. Some think Yeshua is really alluding to the triumphant note at the end of Psalm 22. The innocent sufferer will be vindicated, as in Psalm 22, and as in Yeshua's resurrection and exaltation after the cross.

But Mark's account is realistic about Yeshua's suffering. He is not likely hinting at his coming triumph here. And the idea that Yeshua expected to be saved from the cross goes against so much that has been said. In not being saved Yeshua saves.

The abandonment Yeshua feels is likely real. God has deserted him. This may be understood in more developed theology as having to do with the relation of the Father and the Son. But more simply, in Mark's account, it is the messianic prophet facing punishment and abandonment by God and all others.

A number of confusions and further mockeries ensue. Yeshua's words are reported in Aramaic as well as Greek. This is so Mark can show the reader how it happened that onlookers confused his words as a call for Elijah (*Eli* is short for *Eliyahu*).

An onlooker gives Yeshua sour wine and suggests the crowd should wait and see if Elijah comes. Is his action mockery or some kind of sympathetic aid to Yeshua? In consistency with the story, this is more likely mockery. And the desperately thirsty, dying man drinks the sour wine readily. Yeshua is suffering.

The Shout of Death

Yeshua's final shout is his death, his dying cry (Evans and Wright, 34). Some have seen here a shout of power, that the power of Yeshua is seen in his final cry. The volume of the cry or perhaps some note of triumph in his dying breath is thought to be one of the things that persuaded the centurion just after.

But Yeshua's death has been about not saving himself. Cruelty has gone unanswered. Abandonment has been expressed.

Joel Marcus, in my judgment, goes too far in suggesting that at the moment of his death, Yeshua was possessed by a demon (Gaventa and Hays, 145). But the final cry is more likely anguish than triumph. It may even be that in that moment of crossing over, Yeshua had a deeper insight into the punishment he was bearing. It is not Jerusalem that is being punished but Yeshua. In taking on himself the messianic woes, the tribulation foretold to come, Yeshua is saving his people, not further condemning them. And Yeshua in Mark's account may struggle with the necessity of the brutal path but he does not shrink back. Nor does God comfort him in any way. The shout of Yeshua's death is the lowest moment, the most innocent sufferer experiencing the greatest suffering.

The Temple Curtain

Is this the inner or outer veil, the one before the holiest place or the one visible to onlookers before the golden doors of Herod's Temple?

The transaction on the cross is with God and the inner veil is the one most potently symbolic. It protects the world and Israel from the fatal holiness of God, the very holiness which has just killed Yeshua.

Does this mean the Temple is judged, soon the be destroyed in retaliation for Yeshua's death? Does this mean instead something fortuitous, that the way to God has been opened up for all through Yeshua's death? This meaning, preferred by many, is not likely. Mark's account is not about fortuitous things and Yeshua's kingship is not about triumph but suffering.

We can only guess the meaning of the curtain tearing. Perhaps it is God's anguish being displayed. His righteous one has died unjustly. In more developed theological terms, the Father has given up the Son. The Presence which was over the Ark in the First Temple has been gone for a long time. But the Name of God nonetheless was said to dwell in the Second. It is the place on earth thought of as God's dwelling. And in that place there is destruction. Without guessing too specifically, we can suggest here an appearance of God, a reaction from heaven, and it appears to be an emotional one. He tears his garments in mourning (a common custom in the Ancient Near East and still reflected in modern Jewish mourning rituals). We have to ask if God can mourn and, if so, what does it mean for us when God gives up his own for love?

He is the Son of God!

We might ask dozens of questions about the centurion, how much he did or did not understand Jewish titles and Yeshua. But all these details are secondary to Mark's account. Why did the Roman supervising Yeshua's death say he is the Son of God? What does it mean for Mark's community?

The prevailing theme has been irony. Yeshua is the ironic king. Those calling on him to save himself would deny Israel and the world the salvation that Yeshua's death brings. The innocent sufferer follows the pattern of ancient scriptures and is abandoned by God. The most innocent bears more guilt than any criminal.

The statement of faith by this centurion, whether it is complete and with understanding (indicating that the centurion joined the early Yeshua movement?) or incomplete, a Roman who saw a great man die and imputed to him a kind of demigod status, is the ultimate irony. The disciples will abandon Yeshua just like God. The leaders of Yeshua's nation, the nation he is saving, reject him.

But the one who sees is an instrument of secular power, an oppressor of Israel. He is one who hails Caesar with such titles. Augustus was granted the title Son of God (Evans and Wright, 35). It is a title that would come to other Caesars as well. But this Roman prefigures the confession of the Yeshua movement that this man, this dead criminal, is the Son of God. At this moment, all have left Yeshua. He will have mourners to bury him, but he has no followers now—except one unexpected believer. The darkness is complete. Dawn is coming.

Chapter 16

The Living and Present Lord
Luke 24:1-53

If you were to forget what you know about the resurrection stories and read them with fresh eyes, several things would occur to you as strange. They don't seem to communicate much in the way of inspiration. They don't go on at length about what Yeshua's post-resurrection body was like. They don't speak much about the future, about the renewed world, about every man under his fig tree or white fluffy clouds or any picture at all we've heard of concerning an afterlife. N.T. Wright says it well, "If all we had was the stories of Jesus' crucifixion and resurrection, we would never know that anyone ever interpreted the resurrection narratives as providing a basis for a future hope beyond the grave" (*Resurrection*, 604).

What gives? Shouldn't these stories of defeated death and a raised Messiah brim over with hope, dripping bits of pure light as candles in the darkness of this present age? When there is such an opportunity for preaching, for using stories to proselytize amongst the world-weary Jews and Romans longing for a sign in the dark, why do we get instead perplexity, fear, doubt, uncertainty, and at best a confusing view of Yeshua's state after his raising?

Having considered the options, Wright opts for the view that these stories are based on early accounts, as yet unfiltered (610-15). It is not that they were written early. They are written quite late, most scholars thinking the gospels date to four to six decades after Yeshua rose. There has been a lot of time for theological reflection. In fact, Paul's writings (especially 1 Cor 15), which are much earlier, do overflow with the light of eternal dwellings and the music of the everlasting hills.

But consider each of the four gospel versions of the resurrection and how they appear to be the recollections of stupefied witnesses trying to comprehend. Mark's account is the most uncertain since we do not know how his account originally ended. Any modern translation will tell you that verses past Mark 16:8 were found only in later manuscripts. Assuming that vs. 8 is the original ending of Mark, which is possible, Mark's account is the rawest. The resurrection is not only startling, but leaves the women overwhelmed and afraid.

Matthew's account follows Mark closely (and a good theory is that Mark's original ending may have been similar to Matthew's). Yet he develops the story further, including some stories designed to emphasize that, hard as it is to believe, the empty tomb of Yeshua and the appearances really happened. Yet the most significant happening beyond the empty tomb for Matthew is Yeshua on the mountain in Galilee appointing his disciples to continue his work and spread it.

Luke's account is quite different beyond the empty tomb narrative. His is about Yeshua's appearances in Jerusalem, first secretly and then openly. He reveals two things: that the suffering and resurrection had to happen according to the scriptures and that his living presence will go out through the disciples to Israel and the nations.

John's account beyond the empty tomb focuses on yet other aspects. There are important appearances in Jerusalem and in Galilee (giving credence to Matthew and Luke's versions). John zeroes in more on the unusual nature of Yeshua's post-resurrection body, which has characteristics Wright calls *transphysicality* (477, 606). The fourth gospel, of course, lays stress on faith, but also deals in the final chapter with issues of Peter, the beloved disciple, and the timing of Yeshua's expected return.

What is it about these narratives that makes a leading historian and New Testament scholar to view them as raw, as reflecting early, unvarnished, even puzzled reactions to a virtually inexplicable event? Wright speaks of the strange absences and unusual features of the resurrection narratives under four topics:

- the silence of the Bible
- the absence of personal hope
- the inclusion of women
- the unusual descriptions of Yeshua's body.

The Strange Absences and Features of the Resurrection Narratives

How is it that the resurrection narratives are not peppered with allusions and citations from the Hebrew Bible? Having just left the narratives of Yeshua's trial and death, the reader might expect the same sort of midrashic litany of verses. The innocent sufferer and the servant themes of various biblical texts were combined for Yeshua into a compelling rationale for laying down his life. No such textual rationale is even attempted for the resurrection. Wright notes even more the strangeness of this absence since "as we saw in 1 Corinthians 15:4 . . . from the earliest days of that tradition the resurrection of Jesus was seen as having occurred precisely 'according to the scriptures'" (600).

Further, it is commonplace in Christian theology and in Paul to see a connection between the resurrection of Yeshua and the personal hope of his followers in a resurrected afterlife. In 1 Corinthians 15:17-20, for example, Paul (who wrote well before the gospels were put to writing) centers the hope of Yeshua's followers precisely on the connection that Yeshua's resurrection means resurrection at the end of the age for all his followers.

Look as hard as you like and you won't find this personal hope in the gospel resurrection narratives. As Wright explains:

If all we had was the stories of Jesus' crucifixion and resurrection, we would never know that anyone ever interpreted the resurrection narratives as providing a basis for a future hope beyond the grave. These stories are about something else altogether: the vindication of Jesus, the validation of his messianic claim, and the commissioning of his followers to acts as his heralds, announcing to the world its new, surprising, but rightful lord (604).

Not only are the gospel resurrection narratives not as theologically developed, not as poignantly preachy, as we might expect. They also fail to be properly edited to maximize their credibility. Written four to six decades after the event, you might expect these stories to be touched up, to be edited purely for persuasion as well as inspiration. Yet they are stark, featuring liabilities in their telling.

Not least in these liabilities is the unanimous (all four gospels) agreement that the women who followed Yeshua discovered the empty tomb. In fact, the women come more quickly to believe and understand the import of the empty tomb than the men among Yeshua's disciples. And in the world of that time, especially the Jewish world and also the Roman, women were not acceptable witnesses (607).

Finally, the nature of Yeshua's bodily existence after the resurrection is surprising. Based on the story of the transfiguration and also earlier texts like Daniel 12:3, one might expect Yeshua to appear as a radiant, blinding figure of light. Instead, he has wounds. He walks into locked rooms. He eats. He invites people to touch him. He disappears, moving in some *transphysical* manner which defies the laws of physics that are apparent to us.

When you put these strange absences together, what can you conclude? Wright argues against every other theory but one: the gospel accounts are slavishly, and even detrimentally to their motive of creating belief, faithful to early accounts which are so well known that doctored stories would be recognized as fraudulent. It is as if the writers of these stories were saying, "I didn't understand it [the resurrection] at the time, and I'm not sure I do now, but this is more or less how it was" (611).

Luke's Account: An Overview

There is a core that all four gospels share in the resurrection stories:

- The empty tomb was discovered early on the first day of the week

- Mary Magdalene and other women were the first witnesses
- They found the stone already rolled away
- They saw variously one or two figures thought to be angels.

There is also a core in the three gospels for which we have a certainty about their ending (as opposed to Mark):

- That the women reported to the disciples
- That Yeshua appeared in Jerusalem
- That people touched him
- That Yeshua's primary objective after the resurrection was to appoint his disciples to continue and expand the mission he came for

Luke's account contains all of these elements. It also masterfully develops a number of themes:

- Perplexity, neither the women nor the disciples understood or believed
- Remembrance, that in Yeshua's teaching and in the scriptures this all should have been known in advance
- Mystery, Yeshua's mode of existence is unexplained
- Continuation, Yeshua's living presence will be imparted and the mission will continue and expand

Perplexity

Both the women and the disciples in Luke's account are the powerless observers of a force beyond their ability to comprehend.

The women find the stone too heavy for them to move already rolled out of the way. Yeshua's body, which they came in their own power to anoint, is gone. Two dazzling figures speak to them and the helpless women can only prostrate themselves. The heavenly messengers upbraid them for their lack of faith rather than praising their love for the man Yeshua whom they came to anoint. These angelic beings remind them of Yeshua's words and only then do they remember. The supposedly powerful apostles, closest to Yeshua, hear it from the women. As if this is not enough, the words seem "as nonsense" and the apostles do not believe. Two disciples on the road do not recognize Yeshua who appears to them. The moment they do recognize him, Yeshua disappears and they are helpless again. Even after this, when Yeshua appears to the disciples in Jerusalem, they are terrified and think it is a ghost.

The resurrection of Yeshua is not something to be understood rationally. It is not an event at which observers can be active, in charge. It is something that happens and overwhelms you. It is a fact that precedes understanding, a power that gives meaning rather than an event to interpreted for its meaning. The ways of God are not predictable to the philosopher or even the prophet, for God is the Infinite One whose ways are beyond tracing out.

Remembrance

The perplexity theme might seem to be at odds with the remembrance theme, but actually they can go together in a world where words and even scriptures are viewed as supra-rational.

Luke's account develops the remembrance them more than any other. The women are the first to be reminded. The angelic messengers say, "remember how he told you." They are reminded that Yeshua said in advance (as all four gospels indicate) that the Son of Man would suffer, rise, and be exalted. It is when these words come back to them that the women remember.

The two disciples walking near Jerusalem to Emmaus don't understand it all either. Yeshua is now in their thinking merely a prophet, a good man cut down unfairly. The cloaked and hidden Yeshua rebukes them for not remembering. This time what they are to remember is the Hebrew Bible and the way it validates Yeshua's identity and aims, including the suffering, resurrection, and exaltation. It is not until Yeshua briefly uncloaks himself, when they recognize him for the instant before he literally disappears, that they feel the fire of remembrance: "were not our hearts burning within us?"

The larger group of disciples is, even after this, perplexed when Yeshua appears in Jerusalem. Yeshua rebukes their lack of faith and reminds them too. Almost verbatim as he reminded the two disciples, he now reminds them all. He "opened their minds so they could understand." The supra-rational can come only from revelation, not from unaided reason. The remembrance theme does not indicate that knowing the fact of resurrection from the scriptures and the words of Yeshua makes resurrection rational. Far from it, the words of scripture and Yeshua can communicate the supra-rational. Our minds must be opened to comprehend. Reason is faith seeking understanding, as a famous Christian father would later say.

Mystery

Why didn't the two disciples near Emmaus recognize Yeshua? Was it because they were so conditioned to believe death final? Did it not occur to them that a man who looked like Yeshua could actually be Yeshua? Or was Yeshua's clothing somehow designed to hide his appearance? Or was there some sort of supernatural explanation? Was Yeshua's form changeable or was there mysterious cloaking of the eyes and intellect going on?

One thing we know from the story: the cloaking was deliberate, as it says, "their eyes were kept from recognizing him."

The theme of unrecognition is not the end of the mystery. After an initial conversation, as the two were about to stop, Yeshua indicated he wanted to keep walking and separate from them. They had to urge him to stay, to dine with them, and to talk more. Was it Yeshua's purpose to reveal more to them? If so, why did he pretend to want to go on further? Is this an indication that revelation requires the will of the learner to go deeper?

Yet the mystery continues. As he broke the bread, the two suddenly recognized him. Is this a natural remembrance, because Yeshua had broken bread with his followers so many times before?

Or was some kind of supernatural cloaking brought to an end and Yeshua's form became recognizable at that instant?

Immediately he vanished. How does a person vanish? Is Yeshua tangible or intangible? In the next section he eats fish. Yet he disappears instantly at will. The mystery of Yeshua's post-resurrection body is not something to explain, but to wonder at.

Continuation

When Yeshua appears in Jerusalem, his message is not only remembrance, but also continuation. A certain message which he characterized as "forgiveness of sins" needed proclaiming. Something about what Yeshua had accomplished provided a new opportunity for forgiven sin. This message would be proclaimed "in his name," in the name of Yeshua. It is either that the forgiveness comes in Yeshua's name or the proclamation or both. And the limits of this proclamation are "to the nations." The pattern is from Jerusalem, Zion as the prophets would say, and out to the nations. It may be that already in expounding the Torah and prophets Yeshua has related his accomplishments to the Isaiah prophecies about the Servant bringing the word to the coastlands, the ends of the earth, and the nations.

The disciples will be witnesses. The message cannot be divorced from the occurrences. Forgiveness is because of the things the apostles have witnessed. The inbreaking of God's kingdom is through events in history and not merely through words. Yeshua's accomplishments in the suffering, resurrection, and exaltation are the basis of the continuation and the message. That he died, was raised, and ascended to the throne of high authority at God's right hand is the necessary cause and point of departure.

Yeshua says he is sending what his Father promised. Luke has not developed this theme in depth like the fourth gospel does in chapters 14-16. Yet John the Baptist had foretold a baptism in the Holy Spirit (Luke 3:15-18). Yeshua may be referring to promises from the prophets as well. From what is said later, that this is about "power from on high" and the statements in Acts 1, this is about the empowerment of the Spirit which will be granted to the disciples.

In the fourth gospel, the identity and nature of this Holy Spirit, is further defined in the texts about the Paraclete (Comforter, Advocate), who is the living presence of Yeshua mediated by the Holy Spirit to his followers. Luke does not delve into such details. Yet in Acts, it will become clear that the Spirit empowers these disciples to continue what Yeshua started. So, in a different way, by writing a sequel, Luke does reveal that the Holy Spirit present in the community of Yeshua is Yeshua's Spirit.

And as Yeshua leaves he blesses his disciples. The gift from the Father has not yet come. But the movement is left with Yeshua's blessing. What can it mean for a community to have the blessing of the one who sits at God's right hand? Is that blessing still on us two thousand years later? Are we making use of it?

Much is unexplained and the resurrection story is told without an emphasis on personal hope or afterlife. This story is about something else, something that happened and which overwhelms us. We may be able after the fact to see a connection between Yeshua's resurrection and the hope of our own resurrection, but this story leaves something else burning in our hearts. It is something from of old, a plan of God revealed in the pages of the Hebrew Bible. It is all rather mysterious, cloaked, perplexing, but apparently Yeshua blessed his disciples and promised the gift of Spirit because we are the ones who will fill out the remaining pages. Yeshua is alive, in and through us.

Chapter 17

The True Vine
John 15:1-17

The stories of Yeshua demand a response. The normal order of meaning, the rules of the game called life, are changed in his stories. We are each confronted with the problem of meaning, the possible ways his story intersects our story.

In a number of his sayings, Yeshua says something about himself or about a way of life that calls for action. He implies that when we have encountered him (in our case, through story and not in person), we will understand something about the realm above, about a deeper life, about a breakthrough from the present world to the world to come.

I have said that stories are how we know. Even when we encounter events and persons live and up close, we interpret these encounters in stories. In some cases, with important events, we compare stories later with others who experienced them. We are often surprised at the varying perspectives others have on the same encounters. Their stories never completely match ours. Reality is complicated, capable of viewing simultaneously from multiple perspectives.

In any story we encounter, the main thing we check for is coherence. A friend talks about an encounter with a paranormal experience. Perhaps we are skeptical because we have not had a similar experience. This story seems to break the normal rules, is not coherent with our experience of the world. We may find other stories that are similar by people who are similar and decide that the teller is gullible, biased toward seeing the paranormal without proper evidence.

Many think of Yeshua's stories like this. Maybe the early followers of Yeshua were gullible. Maybe they did not understand the finality of death or the unalterability of disease and disability. They may have been too quick to believe in healed lepers and raised messiahs.

But we have to ask what our standard for belief should be. Should we insist that we see Yeshua ourselves? If we did, would that be enough? Do we insist on personal encounter for every story we believe? What level of coherence would it take for us to accept the Yeshua stories as true (true for us, or however we think of truth)?

Consider some of the revelations of Yeshua about himself or about a way of living life that call for response: Yeshua as healer, as the defeater of demonic powers, as the possessor of the secret to God's kingdom, as the one who dines with sinners, as the Son of Man, as the one with authority on earth to forgive sins, as the founder of a movement to come after him, as the one who gave his life as a ransom, and as the only revealer of the life that is above. Let's consider each of these aspects of Yeshua's story and then consider one last saying of Yeshua, one in which he taught about the ongoing response required by his story.

Yeshua as Healer

In chapter 5, I said that through his many miracles of healing, Yeshua was enacting a foreshadowing of the coming age. In the age to come, disease, disability, and death will not harm anyone any longer. Yeshua brought a small piece of God's kingdom with him wherever he went. People experienced the absence of death.

Our story involves all three of these tragedies of life. We cannot escape them. But Yeshua often said to those he healed, "believe."

If there really is a coming age, a renewed world without tragedy, it changes the way we live our story. One possible response to this idea is to ridicule it. It could be just a way for religious people to let God off the hook for suffering. It could just be a way for the rich to keep the poor content.

Or it could be real. Only you can decide how believable the idea is. Only you can decide how important it is. If it doesn't seem an important concept at the moment, perhaps it will be when you face tragedy. And if you already believe it, many have found it valuable to think of it often and to grow in a deeper vision of its reality day by day.

Yeshua as the Defeater of Demonic Powers

In chapter 4, I said that Yeshua's many clashes with demonic powers, and his total victory over them, was a sign along the way. I noted that encounters with demons never came up with any regularity in biblical literature before Yeshua or after him. Demonic confrontation, if we believe the Yeshua stories, concentrated in and around the life and person of Yeshua.

We can surmise from this that demonic powers do not normally show themselves. For this reason, anti-supernaturalists can easily poke fun at talk of demonic powers. But is the idea really so incredible that, assuming the supernatural exists, that intelligences of evil might be manipulating things behind the scenes in some way?

We see some sort of evil force at work in humanity and in history. What does it mean that Yeshua can defeat these forces? How does it affect our story? We might be humbled by the realization of our own lack of power to overcome the darkness. We might continue the fight to promote justice, love, and peace while realizing that our efforts will never completely succeed. As the sages of Judaism said in *Pirkei Avot*, "You are not expected to complete the work and yet you are not free to desist from it" (2:16). But we can believe that Yeshua will defeat the demonic powers. He opposed them on days one and two, and on the third (his resurrection), he reached the goal.

Yeshua as the Possessor of the Secret to God's Kingdom

In chapter 6, I said that the messianic secret theme in Mark reflected Yeshua's strategy of putting off popular notions of messianic victory so he could teach his inner circle the deeper meaning of his purpose and identity. No crass conqueror, Yeshua sought to enlighten his disciples to a more radical plan of a suffering redeemer, a curse-bearer messiah who would save others from the curse.

In chapter 11, I said that Yeshua engaged his audience with a two-part strategy. He taught in vague parables and similes that drew large crowds to wonder about the age to come and whether Yeshua was a prophet or messiah. But he invited an inner circle, which was open for new people, to linger longer and hear more. To his inner circle Yeshua told and retold the parables of the kingdom in different forms and explanations.

How does Yeshua's possession of the kingdom secrets affect our story? Perhaps we need to hear and rehear Yeshua's words as his inner circle did. Yeshua evoked a sense of immediacy to the paradisiacal aspects of God's kingdom, not just a sense of distance. Perhaps in our circle, with our family and friends, we can and should find ways of making the kingdom of God a reality now to the extent it is possible.

Yeshua as the One who Dines with Sinners

In chapter 9, discussing the story of the Prodigal, I said that Yeshua had a vision of God's boundless and unhesitating forgiveness. He dined with people who occasioned scandal. Those who judged Yeshua in their minds saw him as uncaring about holiness because he did not choose those whom he shared hospitality with according to their standards.

Some have concluded from this that Yeshua cared little about issues of sin and guilt. He offered absolution without contrition, forgiveness for free. Yet he had a way of saying things like, "I have not come to call the righteous, but sinners to repentance" (Luke 5:32).

Yeshua's acceptance of people for what they might become, instead of for what they are, reflects a different view of people. What people are lacking is a connection to the life-giving power of faith in God. We may need to be one of the sinners dining at Yeshua's table as well as entertaining others at our own. Our social habits and desire for higher station in the eyes of others may be causing us to miss out on people who will become important to us. Our ideas about traits that render people valueless may be obstructing us from seeing something beautiful. And perhaps a low view of God's mercy keeps a burden of guilt on our own shoulders that would leave if we saw the boundless, unhesitating forgiveness of the Father as Yeshua did.

Yeshua as the Son of Man

In chapter 6, I said that Yeshua mixed up categories in the minds of his disciples. He said that the Son of Man would suffer. Peter rebuked Yeshua for saying such things. The Son of Man is the one who received the rule of the world from the Ancient of Days. The Son of Man is the king whose rule never ends. The Son of Man will preside over the age to come, when the renewed world will know joy, peace, and love without end.

Yet, God's victories come in unexpected ways. What else should we expect from the Infinite One who can win any way he chooses? He can even win by losing.

The defeat of Yeshua by the leaders of his own nation, by the oppressing power of Rome, and by the powerlessness of his ideas to conquer and reshape a nation is a reason people do not drop everything and follow him today. The world continues on in tragedy and evil. Nothing much has changed since Yeshua came on the scene.

The story of the disciples' shock and dismay at the vanquishing of the Son of Man continues in the faithlessness of people today. Our reality is like theirs.

What possible response can Yeshua's repeated claim to be the Son of Man call for in us? Are we willing to believe in a God who allows the losses to pile up, even terrible things like the dead bodies of children?

But Yeshua's story should make us question our cynicism. He knew the end of his story. Yet he still talked about the coming of the Son of Man to judge the world and rule. Sheep and goats will be separated. The seed of Israel's return from exile will grow into reality. The angels of the Son of Man will renew the world. He will be seen at the right hand of power and then coming with the clouds.

The problems of delay and apparent defeat plague our faith. Are we naive to put hope in a future figure of justice and love?

Yeshua's story makes us confront this issue and ask ourselves what we choose to believe about it.

Yeshua as the One with Authority on Earth to Forgive Sins

We all too easily forget our limitations and imagine ourselves capable of any and all kinds of knowledge. We even fall into judging God (God wouldn't do that, shouldn't allow this, etc.). All such statements are forgivable, but is our presumption of access to the highest forms of knowledge helpful?

We cannot possibly know from our limited perspective what are the barriers to a higher life, to the life of the eons (eternal life) in the presence of God. We have to come to the only one who knows: Yeshua. He has authority on earth to forgive sins, he says in several of the stories we know of him. If he says both that our sins are a barrier between us and God and that he, and only he, has authority to forgive them, do we accept his claim or not?

Yeshua as the Founder of a Movement to Come after Him

In chapter 12, I said the movement Yeshua intended to leave after him was more than a band of disciples. It was a renewed and reconstituted remnant within Israel that would spread out to all Israel and to people from all the nations. It was a mustard seed that would grow large. In chapter 16, I said the disciples were witnesses who would pass down the story of Yeshua and the message of forgiveness of sins for all people, starting in Jerusalem and going to all nations.

In many hints and commandments, Yeshua spoke of the community that would come after him. His living Presence (the Paraclete or Advocate or Comforter) would be with the community. It was to operate as Yeshua's family, his mother and brothers. It was to be a fellowship of mutual sharing and love.

Yeshua's story is not about a private encounter or personal decisions. It is about people of God in community. An individual either remains within the covenant relationship between Israel and God or departs from it. But belonging is corporate. An individual either joins the righteous followers of Yeshua from the nations or remains separate. But belonging is corporate.

Yeshua's story is about more than private faith. It connects us to Yeshua's mother and brothers , who already exist in imperfect and humble communities all around us. Everything Yeshua asks of us ultimately is to be expressed in community.

Yeshua as the One who Gave His Life As a Ransom

In chapter 15, I said the irony of Yeshua's death is that if he saved himself, as his doubters defied him to do, he would not save others. In chapter 14, I said that Yeshua's silence at his trial and his refusal to defend himself against even false charges was a determination to be condemned and to die. Yeshua's deliberate path to the cross is victory through submission, taking a curse to lift a curse.

Yet the *titulus* which hung above Yeshua's head said, "King of the Jews." The irony of Yeshua's death confronts us with the question of meaning. In one place he described his death as a ransom, a payment of a debt (most likely referring to the debt we owe God). Must we understand all the reasons for this odd sort of victory or must we accept it and believe? The example of the Roman centurion calls out to us. Seeing what looked to others like defeat, he cried out what perhaps must be our affirmation too, "Truly this man is the Son of God."

Yeshua as the Only Revealer of the Life That Is Above

In chapter 13, I said that Yeshua was more than a teacher who comes from God. He is the only one who has been in the highest realm who has come down to show us how to be born from above. He is the only one, he claimed, who can infuse us with the life of the eons, with union with God.

Our view of God and life with God is necessarily too low, because as finite persons we cannot comprehend infinitude. Yeshua explained that to be made ready for life in its highest form, we required a supernatural change, something the prophets had variously described as heart circumcision, divine cleansing with water, a new heart and spirit, and a Torah written on our hearts.

Yeshua claimed to be the radiance emanating from the direct being of God, the Son who emanates from the Father. In later Jewish terminology, we could say that Yeshua is the sum of the *sefirot* (emanations of Presence) coming from the *Ein Sof* (the Without End, the Infinite One). Yeshua is the Presence of God we can grasp and the Father is the Infinite One who is beyond knowing.

This is Yeshua's story. He came down, he said, to be lifted up and in so doing bring us up to the life that is above. That life will be here on earth. It is physical and spiritual, just as we are physical and spiritual. So Yeshua could say to his followers that whoever had seen him had seen the Father. He could say that he would bring us to be with him where he will be. He could say that he came to bring his peace and joy to us.

Do we accept this view of God as infinitely beyond us? Do we accept this view that the Presence (also described in other texts as the Word, the Name, the Glory, the Wisdom, and the Image of God) is Yeshua and that he came to bring us transformation and birth?

The Solitary Source

In his final discourses with his disciples, Yeshua told a parable, a twist on an old theme of the vineyard (see Isa 5; Jer 2; Ezek 15, 17, and 19). The parable is fully told in John 15:1-4 and its meaning is expounded in vss. 5-17.

The characters are a gardener, a vine, branches on the vine, and fruit. The gardener is the Father, God in his direct being, the Infinite One. The vine is the Presence, the Son, the one who emanates from the Father, Yeshua. Some branches are removed and others are cleaned, an odd word choice for pruning which is deliberately chosen to play off of vs. 3 ("you are clean already").

I have chosen this story to wrap up this exploration of the life and times of Yeshua because Yeshua used it as a legacy story, telling his disciples what to do after him. Some elements of the story are notoriously vague, so ambiguous people have not been sure what Yeshua's specific teaching was about, what action his followers are to take.

A helpful realization is that vss. 1-4 tell the whole story and vss. 5-17 expound on their meaning. Yeshua's teaching has the following elements:

- The Yeshua movement is like branches on a vine. The vine is Yeshua and the planter is the Father.

- The Father is the ultimate judge, removing branches that will be fruitless. The fruit is not yet defined. The meaning of being removed is not clear.

- The disciples are clean, already pruned, because they have witnessed and heard Yeshua's word. The exact contents of this word are not defined as yet.

- The main command or wisdom for the disciples and the whole Yeshua movement to come is that they remain in Yeshua. That is, they need to not be removed. The key to remaining is apparently two-fold: being made clean by the word from Yeshua and bearing fruit so as not to be removed by the Father.

- Yeshua is the solitary source of the life and nourishment required to bear the mysterious fruit. It is as pointless to go on without Yeshua as for a grape branch to attempt fruit-bearing after being removed from the life of the vine.

The Vine and the Vineyard

In the prophets, Israel is a vineyard planted by God. They started as a choice vineyard, but wild grapes took over. Fruit was scarce. The vineyard was disappointing. Several other images of the vineyard and Israel as the vine populate the prophets. The imagery is loose. Israel can be the vineyard or the vine. Too much should not be read into details. The point is that God is like the planter of a community from which he hopes to receive a harvest of goodness and plenty.

The disciples are not a replacement for Israel, but, as the gospels and Acts develop the theme, a seed of life and renewal in the midst of Israel. They are a renewal remnant from within destined to spread to all Israel and to the nations into a divinely made people from Israel and the nations. The planter is the Father, but a new development is introduced into the usual image: the Father planted a vine which is his Presence in the world, the Son who reveals the Father. And the Israelites and righteous of the nations are branches on the vine of the Presence.

The Father Who Removes

Removing excess branches after the growing season is essential. Excess wood reduces the fruit of a vine. They are cut back mercilessly.

What causes a branch to be removed? It does not bear fruit and it does not remain in Yeshua. The first is explained in vs. 2 and the second in vs. 6. Removed branches are useful only as fuel for the fire. This is read by many as an image of hell, a suggestion that removed branches are burned up. Yet there are reasons to doubt this.

First, there is no specific statement about judgment in the afterlife here. The assumption that the burning of the branches is an image of hell is an assumption without evidence. Second, we know that branches that are not in Yeshua at some point enter into Yeshua. That God can give life to dead branches and join them to the vine whenever he wants is without question. Third, the point of the image is the uselessness of the disconnected branches, so that they are only fuel. What we can discern for certain from Yeshua's teaching is that removed branches are not connected to the solitary source. They are unable to bear fruit in the ultimate sense. They are apart from Yeshua and seeking to do things on their own (vss. 4-5).

To be removed is to be apart from Yeshua, missing the solitary source of life and fruit. It is a state in this life, not the life to come. The life to come is not the subject of this parable at all.

Clean Because of the Word of Yeshua

The disciples are clean, already pruned, because they heard the word of Yeshua. The word of Yeshua is clarified further in vss. 5-17. The word is about the commandments of Yeshua (vs. 10). Yeshua gave these commandments so the disciples would have complete joy as Yeshua has joy (vs. 11). The commandment is to form a community of mutual love (vss. 12, 17). The ultimate example for this community is what Yeshua is about to do, lay his life down as a sacrifice for his friends (vs. 13). The disciples, inasmuch as they obey and form this community as commanded are Yeshua's friends (vs. 14), no longer servants but friends with a full revelation of the Father (vs. 15). They did not choose Yeshua, but were chosen by him, as those who would form such a community of mutual love (vs. 16).

The word of Yeshua is the sum of all the disciples have learned from being with Yeshua. They have seen him heal and defeat demonic powers. They know the kind of life that will be in the world to come. They are to form a community with such an existence. In their community, mourners will be comforted, the hungry will be filled, the poor will be blessed. They will love each other with sacrificial, redemptive love.

There is no such thing as being a solitary follower of Yeshua. His commandment requires inclusion in a community defined by love. All other branches are removed.

Remaining in the Vine

The meaning of "remain in me," then, is not vague or difficult to comprehend. It means to believe the word Yeshua lived and spoke and to follow through by belonging to the community formed in Yeshua's name. Inasmuch as we who are disciples of the disciples include ourselves in Yeshua's communities, as poor as they may seem, as imperfect and far removed from the glories of the ideal life Yeshua taught, we are doing, as best we can, to remain in Yeshua. And his living presence is with us, mystically, inaudibly, and invisibly.

What about the rest of the branches? Are the people of Israel dead off the vine? Are those from the nations who are not members of Yeshua's community without hope?

There is hope in the very image of a vine and a gardener. Israel is and always will be God's vineyard. God disciplines but does not cast off Israel. So there must be hope for all cut off branches. How far that hope extends and where all hope is lost is not a part of this tale.

The point of Yeshua's story is not speculation about the afterlife and who will be included. It is about realizing the life of the world to come in this life. Final destinies will be decided by the Father. But the larger issue for those unconnected to the vine is the life they are missing now. And the message for the branches is to remain, to focus on Yeshua's commandment and form communities of mutual love dedicated to all Yeshua stood for, lived out, and taught.

The vineyard has many unhealthy branches. The vineyard has borne too little fruit. The vineyard will attract more branches to be grafted in as the singular focus of Yeshua's word is made alive again. The meaning of Yeshua's life is simple and yet mystical. Yeshua's joy, referred to in vs. 11, is the joy of mutual love with the complex persons of the being of God (Father, Son, and Spirit in eternal relationship, see John 17:5, 24). The joy that God's Emanation, His Presence, has in union with his Spirit and with his direct being is available to all of us branches. The life of God exists within the Yeshua community, the new family of Messiah, his mothers and brothers. The meaning of this life, this joy, this love will ever occupy us.